THE WORLD REBUILT

By the same Author

INNOCENT MEN
FIGHTERS EVER
IDEAS HAVE LEGS
MEN ON TRIAL
THAT MAN FRANK BUCHMAN

THE WORLD REBUILT

*The True Story
of Frank Buchman
and the achievements
of Moral Re-Armament*

by

PETER HOWARD

DUELL, SLOAN AND PEARCE
New York

FIRST PUBLISHED IN THE UNITED STATES SEPTEMBER 1951
FIFTH PRINTING NOVEMBER 1952

TRANSLATED IN NINE LANGUAGES AND PUBLISHED
IN GREAT BRITAIN, GERMANY, FRANCE, ITALY,
BRAZIL, NORWAY, SWEDEN, DENMARK, FINLAND,
SWITZERLAND, THE NETHERLANDS AND CANADA
TOTAL PRINTING ALL COUNTRIES 645,000 COPIES

PRINTED IN THE UNITED STATES OF AMERICA

CONTENTS

•

Part One

Part Two. DOCUMENTS

Part One

I. AMERICA: THE AIRLINES LEAD THE WAY

•

I

"At the start of 1951 you could have bought the good will of our airline for a thousand dollars," said one of the Board of National Airlines. "Today you could not buy it for millions."

A feud which had lasted years, caused one of the longest strikes in airlines history, and was about to cause another one "was brought to a screeching halt as the result of Moral Re-Armament." So says W. T. "Slim" Babbitt, vice-president of the Air Line Pilots Association of America (ALPA).

Two men were at the heart of this feud. One was Babbitt himself, the other G. T. Baker, president of National Airlines.

"We were two deadly enemies," says Slim Babbitt.

Baker is tough and square, a man who has fought his way up from the ground to the top of a large industrial enterprise. He was born in the Middle West with little in his pocket, but with a passion for flying in his heart. He began operating a one-man air service between Chicago and some of the Southern states. Then he moved to Florida and painfully, steadily, resolutely built up the enterprise known as National Airlines. It was a struggle every inch of the way, and in that struggle Baker became ruthless.

Slim Babbitt is a shrewd, down-to-earth character. His language is full of color and life. He is skilled in the art of industrial negotiation and he has fought without fear or favor for the interests of the pilots.

The trouble in National Airlines began many years ago, and distrust, fear, and hate mounted steadily.

Matters came to a head in February 1948, when Baker fired a pilot without, as the pilots believed, giving him a fair chance to state his case. The National pilots went on strike and it became one of the bitterest strikes in airline history.

Baker tried to keep going by introducing non-union pilots.

The union pilots struck back in many ways. Streamers were drawn by planes over Miami and other cities saying, "Don't fly National." Match books were distributed in hotels and on other lines with the same slogan. The offices of National Airlines were picketed and passengers intending to fly National were warned by the striking pilots that the aircraft were unsafe and that the non-union pilots were unskilled men.

The situation between the pilots and National Airlines had come to the point of complete breakdown.

In airfields as far away as Cairo, propaganda against National Airlines was distributed by the striking pilots and their friends.

Baker filed a $5,000,000 claim against them for defaming his company.

After ten months of strike and hatred, the Civil Aeronautics Board stepped in. They ordered an investigation to consider the dismemberment of National Airlines and the dividing up of its services among other airlines.

Finally Baker agreed to put the ALPA pilots back to work and the strike was officially ended. But, in fact, the period between 1948 and 1951 was, to quote Slim Babbitt, "much worse than the actual strike."

In that period the war between Baker and the pilots was waged relentlessly.

Pilots who had played a leading part in the strike were summoned for medical examination by doctors employed by Baker, and pronounced unfit to fly. Then Babbitt would have them re-examined by other doctors, employed by ALPA, who declared they were in sound health.

The pilots, because they hated Baker, would fly National planes in such a way that the riding was bumpy. Then, when passengers complained, they would advise them to travel on other airlines.

Also the pilots sometimes ran the engines of the planes on a very rich mixture so that thousands of gallons of gasoline were wasted.

Babbitt says that in the two years 1949 and 1950 the Pilots' Association spent hundreds of thousands of dollars in their efforts to ruin Baker, "to say nothing of the hundreds of man-hours spent trying to hold our position and out-figure our adversary's next move."

Baker comments, "That is duplicate for me."

At the end of 1950, Babbitt and the pilots decided to put National Airlines and Baker out of business forever. The dismemberment order by the Civil Aeronautics Board was still pending, following the first strike, and in December 1950 Babbitt called the pilots of National to a strike vote, which in his mind meant the end of the airline.

Newspapers published news of this strike vote on the front page.

It is at this point that Moral Re-Armament enters the story. A businessman in Florida, who knows Moral Re-Armament but did not know Baker, decided that the two must be brought together. Executives in the airlines told him it would be impossible for him to see Baker. One of them said, "Why, if the President of the United States wanted to see Baker, Baker would maybe offer him a date for a month ahead and then the secretary would telephone and stall him."

But the businessman was undaunted. He went right to Baker's office and persisted. Finally he came face to face with him. He said, "I see in the papers that you have another strike on your hands." Baker answered, "Yes, we do. And there's not one damned thing you or I or anyone can do about it. We've been through one strike and will go through another.

The question to be settled is whether labor or management is going to run this company." Then he threw his arms in the air and remarked, "What the hell difference does it make? The Communists are on their way to running labor and in a few years they'll get the whole country if things go on like this."

The businessman began to tell him of the world effects of Moral Re-Armament. He spoke of industrial deadlocks in every continent which were being resolved as management and labor began to think and act in terms of "What is Right" instead of "Who is Right."

He spoke of the statesmanship of ordinary men, who, instead of pointing the finger at the other fellow and waiting for him to change his attitude, began to be honest about the places where wrong had displaced right in their own conduct.

Baker said later of this interview, "I was waiting for the gimmick, but it never came. I thought it was some gimmick labor was using to get me down. I thought I would be asked to pay dues or to join something. But it never happened. I began to see there was such a thing as a man who just wants to help. Just the difference between right and wrong. It sounded so damned simple, yet it was so doggone profound."

That afternoon Baker came into the office of the Vice President of National Airlines every fifteen or twenty minutes. His mind had begun to move at a new level. He said, "We haven't been honest. I always thought I was an honest-to-God sort of a guy—but absolute honesty, that's something different. We've pushed these pilots around, you know. We've met together in this room, as heads of management, and we've thought of everything we could that would be in the interests of management, but not one time have we thought what would be in the interests of the pilots. We always thought of what we could get out of it. We haven't been honest with ourselves or with them. This is something brand-new, this MRA. It has changed my thinking a lot."

Word reached Slim Babbitt of a new attitude in Baker. He did not believe one word of it. He sent some of the negotiating pilots around to the National Airlines offices to see what was going on.

They arrived, not expecting to see Baker, but as soon as he heard they were there he sent word to bring the pilots up to his office. They had never been there before. Presently one of them telephoned Babbitt and said, "Where do you think we are? Baker is out of the room at the moment but we are in his office, smoking his cigars. We are four feet off the ground and Baker's on the ceiling and we can't get him down. What is going on over here, anyway?"

Baker proposed to Babbitt that the mediation on the pending strike, fixed for January 2 by the National Mediation Board, should be postponed until after the Moral Re-Armament Assembly which was being held in Washington during the opening days of January 1951, and that Babbitt and some of the pilots should attend the Assembly with Baker and some of his senior executives and see whether a solution could be found.

Babbitt was suspicious. "I thought it would be some kiss-and-make-up stuff to give the pilots the run-around," he said. But he was shaken by Baker's changed attitude. He said. "Baker started to give us so much rope we did not know what to do with it." Finally he said to the pilots, "Now, don't fall out of your chairs or get the wrong idea. We ain't wearing halos or going around in white robes looking saintly. But a firecracker has been lit and it's going off all over the place. For the first time it looks like we might have a chance to sit down and talk with Baker, and I am in favor of postponing mediation and going to the MRA Assembly at Washington."

So it was agreed. But Babbitt was still wary. "I went strictly to case the joint," he says. He would not stay at the same Washington hotel as Baker and the other delegates.

But they met after the performance of one of the MRA plays. Except in the courtroom, during hearings of the cases in which they had fought each other, this was the first time the men had met personally. They went to a hotel room and talked. "We got further in three hours than we had in the three previous years," they later said.

In the atmosphere of the Washington Assembly, attended by fifteen hundred delegates representing government, industry, and labor from twenty-five countries, Babbitt and Baker began to talk about the world situation. Then there was a pause. Baker suddenly said, "I have been wrong. I want to let you know that." He began to tell Babbitt of the places where he felt he had failed to do the right thing in his dealings with the pilots. "He did not blame the pilots once," said Babbitt, "on any point at all. He took full responsibility for everything that had happened. I felt as confused as the kid who dropped his bubblegum in the hen house. Then Baker went on to mention specific cases. He offered to pay a whole year's back salary to one pilot he had victimized. I just felt Baker was giving everything. So I had to do something about it. It was up to me."

Babbitt admitted to Baker that he had "dreamed up" many of the thirteen strike grievances that were at issue as part of the campaign to ruin Baker. He then and there adjusted a claim for promotions not received and loss of wages, so bringing the claim to the right figure.

Baker and his executives, Babbitt and the pilots flew back to Florida. Babbitt wired the Moral Re-Armament Assembly at this time, "We are now busily engaged in the mechanics of cutting the ropes which have retarded National Airlines as well as its pilots so the two will be free to go forward as a team to build an airline with unlimited potentiality for both parties. Until I get more information, I shall refer to MRA as a wonder drug that makes real human beings out of people."

Through February and March 1951, Baker and Babbitt worked together to "cut the ropes" and plan the mechanics of a settlement.

In March they announced their settlement to the press. Baker said, "A whole new factor was brought into the situation through Moral Re-Armament. The real trouble has been bitterness and lack of trust between us. It took an apology and honesty on my part to restore a basis of confidence. . . . I have not always seen the pilots as people. I feel my job now is to return to the pilots the sense of dignity and security to which they are entitled."

Babbitt said the pilots recognized the new approach on the part of management and are "striving to prove the merit of this way of thinking." He added, "If the management and pilots of National Airlines continue to work as a team, as they have been doing this past ninety days, this will be one of the most successful airlines in the country and known in the piloting profession as one of the best with which to be associated."

Following the new spirit in National, the Civil Aeronautics Board withdrew its pending dismemberment order. The banks, which for years had been reluctant to advance money to National, loaned enough to buy a number of new planes.

These events made front-page news. The *Miami Herald* headlined its story: "Moral Re-Armament Ushers in Era of Understanding."

The *Miami Daily News*, commented editorially: "There was none of the familiar emphasis on hard-won bargaining victories. The emphasis was on the moral re-armament of the participants in the dispute."

The *Miami Labor Citizen*, American Federation of Labor, for three consecutive weeks carried stories of Moral Re-Armament across the eight columns of its front page. Editorially this newspaper said of MRA, "It looks good to us as the all-out cure for a very sick world. It is the answer for harmony in the home, it is the answer for labor-management disputes, it is the answer to world-wide discord. . . Moral Re-Armament, to us, is a challenge to all of America."

The settlement of the feud between Baker and Babbitt did

not, of course, mean that all grievances were ended for all time in National. It did mean that an industrial bottleneck which was killing the line was broken.

Baker, commenting on the end of the feud, stated: "Based on our experiences with Moral Re-Armament, there are few industrial conflicts that cannot be solved. The keys to this solution are the application by both management and labor of the four cardinal principles of MRA—absolute honesty, purity, love and unselfishness."

Babbitt, writing to the membership of the ALPA about these four points, said, "A lot of you fellows who have known me for a long time are perhaps thinking, 'How in the hell did Slim qualify on *any* of these points?' Well, you can change, can't you? Before you fellows get any idea that Babbitt's horizon has tumbled or that his gyro is spinning or that he has been drinking compass fluid, I want to say that I am by nature a skeptic and always have been. You know—one of those guys that is always looking at the collection plate in church figuring the thing has two bottoms, the house getting forty per cent and the guy passing it getting the balance. . . . I strongly urge you and your families to . . . find out what tremendous force could bring two deadly enemies to settle their differences of many years' standing in a matter of almost minutes, and also the force that could cut ALPA's expense on National down to practically nothing. ALPA's expense is your money."

D. W. Rentzel, Chairman of the Civil Aeronautics Board, issued the following public statement: "The sudden settlement of the protracted conflict between the management and the Air Line Pilots Association pilot group of National Airlines came as a pleasant shock to the aviation industry.

"The Moral Re-Armament movement deserves major credit for this gratifying development. . . . To those familiar with the long history of bitter and acrimonious dispute the transformation in the attitude of the parties from one of suspicion and hostility to an attitude of mutual co-operation and trust has been little short of miraculous. In effecting a settlement of this bitter struggle Moral Re-Armament has performed an invaluable service, not only to the aviation industry, but to the country as a whole, in pointing the way toward a solution of the broader problem of labor management relations."

II

Following the news made by National Airlines, a task force of Moral Re-Armament was invited to Miami, Florida, by representatives from several of the great airlines.[1] Miami is a strategic center of the airlines industry. All Eastern, Pan American (Latin American Division), and National aircraft are serviced there. Pan American alone employs 4,600 men in Miami. Eastern employs 3,300 there.

Night after night in the Dade County Auditorium audiences of over two thousand saw the idea of Moral Re-Armament displayed on the stage with drama and music. More than twenty-five thousand people saw the plays.[2] The radio and television stations in the space of seven weeks broadcast forty-three programs on MRA. The newspapers published 101 articles.

Eastern Air Lines, Pan American World Airways, and National Airlines arranged a series of training sessions for management, pilots, and workers on company time and at company expense, to learn how to apply Moral Re-Armament in industry. Florida Power and Light Company also made arrangements for 1,800 of their employees to be trained in Moral Re-Armament. In addition, five thousand of the general public attended training sessions.

Leaders of the CIO and the AFL gave these companies backing. When Pan American World Airways gave an MRA Family Night at the Dade County Auditorium, the unions and management jointly issued the invitation and the unions

---

[1] See Document 1, "Melting the Iron Curtain," an address of welcome by Representative William S. Lantaff.
[2] See Document 2, "Jotham Valley" by George E. Sokolsky.

took up a collection to provide funds for the work of Moral Re-Armament.

The combined union-management committee of Pan American said in the program: "The task force of Moral Re-Armament has in a few short weeks in Miami opened the eyes of thousands. They have given us a new approach to the problems which constantly threaten the efficiency and even the life of the Pan American 'team.' We are convinced that the principles they advocate can eliminate the overhead of friction and bring substantial benefits to us all. By accepting the challenge to make MRA a basis for our living at home and on the job, the airlines can give a pattern to industry for the nation and the world.

Typical of the ways in which this pattern to industry was hammered into reality are the following stories.

The chief shop steward of the Engine Overhaul Department of Pan American says: "Before this MRA group came in there was a strong wedge between the personnel on the floor and the management group. Our policy was to go in and win grievances regardless."

After meeting MRA he apologized to his leading opponent. "Now," he says, "our grievances are handled on an entirely different basis, right on the floor with the crew and the foreman. The majority of fellows in that building no longer feel they are a number on a clock but feel a part of the company. Instead of keeping production low, we want to expand production and make it a good company. On our maintenance cost analysis sheets its tells you how efficient your crew is. Three weeks ago we were doing pretty good. We were about 70%. But, through practicing these standards of MRA, the efficiency sheet last week had gone up to 99%."

In another airline, the senior foreman of the electrical shop was regarded by both management and labor as a difficult man. After seeing the MRA plays this foreman said, "Everywhere I operate I am in a fight. I guess the trouble must be me."

He began to change by getting honest with his wife ("She told me she knew all the time anyway," said the foreman) and apologizing to another man for the way he had treated him.

Then the foreman called in twenty of his men to talk to them about MRA.

The session, scheduled for an hour and a half, went on for four hours. One man referred to a fight he and the foreman had had a few days before about the length of time needed to do a check on a DC-3. "You told me it takes ten hours," said the foreman. "I knew perfectly well it doesn't take ten hours, because I used to do it myself." "You told me it only takes four hours," said the man. "I know perfectly well that it can't be done in four hours. Perhaps you could do it years ago, but not now." The two men looked at each other. The foreman smiled, "I am willing to bet that if you and I go away and ask ourselves honestly what is right," he said, "we will come back with figures that are not very far apart."

The man agreed and added, "I've been thinking about all the hours that these battles between us have cost the company." Apologies were made all around and a new co-operation throughout the department was begun.

At the end of a month it was discovered that the number of man-hours which had to be devoted to settling grievances and problems between management and union had dropped from the usual forty to only five.

The foreman got together the whole department for a day of MRA training. "You all know of the trouble between me and the union," he told them. "But you may not know how it started."

He described how he and the man who was now head of the union had driven to work together during the war when both were just workers on the line. They both had explosive temperaments and argued incessantly. Finally the foreman had ordered him out of the car.

"Every time one of you shop stewards has come in about a

grievance," he told them, "you have had to fight through the antagonism in me against that man. It had nothing to do with the question on hand. Now he and I have cleared matters up. We've found in MRA something we can agree on and we're friends."

The foreman had put his finger on a truth which was proved over and over again in Miami with the airlines. The most difficult industrial relations are simple human relations. And they get straightened out as people get straightened out.

Captain Eddie Rickenbacker, President of Eastern Air Lines, speaking at a performance of one of the MRA plays said, "It is my hope and conviction that some day, through the efforts of men and women like you of Moral Re-Armament, instead of spending billions and billions and hundreds of billions of the world's wealth for the destruction of mankind, those billions will be spent for the welfare of man."

Speaking to an outdoor mass meeting of his 2,500 employees, Captain Rickenbacker said, "The only satisfaction I get out of life any more is to see you members of the Eastern family grow in every way. I want you to grow not only financially and mentally but morally. Unless we grow morally, mental and financial growth won't last. If you and I can take the one fundamental principle of Moral Re-Armament—honesty—and live up to that, the other three—purity, unselfishness, and love—will follow. Our ambition is to build leadership of the quality Moral Re-Armament is teaching. If everyone of us could overnight put this spirit into action it would guarantee America would be sure to survive."

III

In the first ten days of June 1951, three hundred and eighty-nine airlines personnel flew in to Pellston Airport at the northern tip of Michigan. They took ship and joined the other thirteen hundred delegates from thirty-two nations at the Moral Re-Armament World Assembly at Mackinac Island.

Eastern, National, and Pan American sent five special planes from Miami, while Pan American (Pacific-Alaska) sent another from San Francisco. Other personnel came from California Eastern, Canadian Pacific, Trans Canada, KLM, Swissair, and BOAC. Every grade from vice-president to porter was represented in the party—pilots, stewardesses, fitters, foremen, executives, clerks, mechanics, and their union leaders.

They came to tell a story which has already affected to the tune of millions of dollars the future of some of the airlines and is fast spreading to others and throughout the industrial life of America and the world.

Mr. William Grogan, International Vice-President of the Transport Workers Union of America and its chief Miami officer, spoke from the platform with Mr. H. W. Toomey, General Manager of the Latin American Division of Pan American. "We were preparing for a world-wide strike when Moral Re-Armament came in," he said. "With all the millions of dollars they spent before, Pan American never got the results that they have had from the few thousand dollars they have spent so far on MRA." Toomey said that Pan American had backed MRA not only because it produced results, but because it was right. He added, "Any management that does not foster and invest in MRA is unenlightened and obsolete. Management must create an environment in industry wherein constructive labor leadership can freely function."

Both men spoke of the personal happiness which MRA had brought to them. "This morning I went to confession and received communion for the first time for eight years," said Grogan. "It took Frank Buchman to make me a good Catholic." And his wife, looking at her husband and the new light in his eye, said, "Today, after twenty-seven years of marriage, I have become the happiest woman in the world."

Let Slim Babbitt sum up in his own words: "The age of MRA is less than the airplane. The atom bomb is less than six years old. All three, you might say, have been available for the use of mankind since the beginning of time. Every ingredient of the airplane, the atom bomb, and MRA have been here since Adam out-negotiated Eve. It was just a case of getting them into a working form. The record of MRA around the world is just as factual and real as any airplane aloft today. While I am just peering over the horizon of MRA myself, these people have really got something workable."

II. WASHINGTON RESPONDS

•

I

At noon on January 15, 1951, two hundred and twenty-five of the international force of MRA sat with Frank Buchman in the gallery of the United States Senate as the day's business began.

They had spent the first days of the year in Washington at a World Assembly, which had drawn leaders from all over the United States and from twenty-five other countries. The theme of the assembly had been, "An ideology that can win the world"—and the visitors had given compelling evidence that a practical answer had been found to Communist strategy in Germany, France, and Italy; to class war in the docks and mines of Britain; to Franco-German disunity; and to the perils of a militant ideology in the Far East.

During these days many congressional leaders had attended sessions in Washington's Shoreham Hotel. Now the MRA force had been invited to the Senate to hear the nation's tribute to their work.

As the business of the day began, many Senators were on their feet asking for the recognition of the Chair. The first was H. Alexander Smith of New Jersey, who said, "America more than ever needs to develop ideological strength if we are to win what is primarily a struggle for the minds of men and women. These men and women merit our attention and support."

Other Senators followed. Then, at the suggestion of the

Chairman of the Foreign Relations Committee, Senator Tom Connally of Texas, Senator Wiley asked and received the Senate's permission for the visitors to rise and be recognized in view of the ("tremendous work they are doing to stabilize the thinking and the living of the people of the world.") As Frank Buchman and his friends rose in the gallery, the Senators broke into applause.

A few days earlier the House of Representatives had paid their tribute. "How many millions—perhaps even billions— might be saved this Government if such a spirit were multiplied throughout the land," declared Representative E. E. Cox of Georgia on that occasion. "It is encouraging indeed at a time when we are compelled to appropriate billions of dollars and mobilize millions of men to meet the threat of world Communism that evidence should be presented in our midst of a burgeoning world force which is answering Communism in men's hearts and minds. Through the capture of key leadership in critical areas this force has actually turned the tide of Communism in some of the most vital danger spots in Europe and Asia."

During the Assembly the MRA force was received by Speaker Rayburn together with House Majority Leader McCormack [3] and Minority Leader Martin and by Vice President Barkley. Members of the Armed Services Committee of the Senate spent an hour and three quarters hearing evidence from the military leaders from Europe, and many others drew upon the expert knowledge which MRA had brought to their doors.

The former Communists from the Ruhr were closely questioned. One of them, who had been for twenty-five years a member of the Communist Party, spoke of the uniting power of MRA between classes and nations. "The unity of the West would be more powerful than an atom bomb on the Kremlin," he said. "Communists do not mind however much the West

[3] See Document 3, "The Rise of a New Spirit," speech by Representative John W. McCormack.

rattles the saber. They know that the Western world can bristle with arms, but without an ideology it will go under. And if, in the case of war, the West were victorious and marched right through to Vladivostok, what happens then?"

"America," said Frank Buchman, "needs an idea in her head and an answer in her heart as well as a gun in her hand."

II

Deeds as well as words made their impact on Washington during the Assembly. Men began to live the idea that they wanted to give America and the world.

Here is the story of one Congressman. He is middle-aged, a typical, average Congressman. He comes from a middle-class family and runs a moderate-sized business in his home town.

He went to one of the Moral Re-Armament plays during the Assembly. Then he and his wife invited several members of the cast to a meal. One girl told them of the revolution that began in the life of her own family and her father's business as a result of a remark she herself made at breakfast one morning: "Daddy, why is it that when you have finished talking, there never seems anything else left to say?"

The Congressman began to think. He asked his wife whether since he had been away at Washington, while she carried on his business at home, there had been less friction in the family. He was astonished at her answer. She said, "Well, if you want to know, dear, I must confess there *has* been less friction."

For the rest of the evening, the Congressman said nothing. Then he took the decision that if he wanted to see America and the world different, the place to begin was with himself.

He wrote a letter to his children, two girls and a boy, in which he was honest with them. He told them that he had been pilot, co-pilot, navigator, radio operator, bombardier, and even steward in the family. He asked their forgiveness.

One daughter, when this letter was received, said to her

mother, "What's the matter with Daddy? I received the strangest letter from him. He has never written like this before. Daddy must be cracking up. It sounds like his last will and testament." Later this girl said, "Even a high-school senior has quite a number of problems, temptations, and wrongs to right. Before, I didn't have courage enough to stand for the very highest of morals with my gang at school. Now I'm not afraid any longer. I quit smoking and necking on dates. I have been absolutely honest with Mother and Daddy about these things. I am now living a life I always wanted to live down deep, but never had the stuffin' to do before. Also, I now have a real purpose for living such a life."

The other daughter had for several years been going from one specialist to another with a severe back ailment. The expense had been heavy, with no cure. Shortly after her father's letter came, she threw away a surgical board she had been sleeping on for three years, and asked for some golf clubs. She now plays golf without trouble.

The Congressman saw how he had been teaching his own son to become a liar. While discussing with his family and disapproving the corruption and immorality that the Kefauver investigation revealed, he found his boy, when answering the telephone, would put his hand over the mouthpiece and shout, "Daddy, some guy wants you. Are you in or out?"—to which the Congressman would reply, "Oh, tell him I will be in at, say, five o'clock."

The Congressman began to train his son to be truthful in everything.

He got honest himself with his wife about money. Through their twenty-four years of marriage he had made enough money, yet they always seemed to be pressed. He had not been honest about his spending, and told his wife so. The wife answered in a letter telling him of some debts which she had contracted and about which the Congressman knew nothing.

At the Congressman's suggestion, the wife took over the budget for all the household. A united plan was worked out which took care of every problem. In addition, husband and wife decided, with the children, to contribute fifty dollars a month to MRA.

One morning at his office on Capitol Hill, the Congressman lost his temper when he found his staff gossiping instead of working. He made a scene. Presently he rang the bell for the secretary, but her hand was shaking so much, following his outburst, that she scarcely could take down the words he was dictating. The Congressman, through his contact with MRA, had learned the secret of listening quietly first thing each morning, to find the mind of God on his life and the life of his community and nation. Next morning he wrote down on a sheet of paper the idea of what was the right thing to do.

On arriving at his office he called in all his staff and said to them, "I lost my temper with you yesterday. I am sorry for it. I was wrong. Please forgive me." When his secretary came into the room later, she said to him, "I want you to know I have been in government service in Washington for fifteen years. I never saw or heard anything like the thing you said to us this morning. I want to thank you."

Since that time, the Congressman says, his office staff have turned out more work with less strain and effort. They are less tired. There is a new atmosphere in the office.

Early one morning the Congressman had another idea. He wrote a letter to the cabinet of a foreign power. In it he told them how wrong motives had dictated certain public action he had once taken in regard to their nation. So he began to build unity between America and the world.

In the story of this Congressman are three elements.

First, the *decision* to fight for what is right.

Second, the *discipline* of applying absolute moral standards to life and accepting change where change is needed.

Third, the *direction* of God sought as the guide of every public and private action.

III

Shortly after the Washington Assembly news came that
Frank Buchman was among those nominated for the Nobel
Peace Prize of 1951.

Men everywhere were looking for a way out of the world
crisis. As that great American Catholic layman, Mr. Joseph
Scott of Los Angeles, said at the Assembly:

"The races of the world are here. I have twenty grand-
children. In their blood they represent both sides of the Irish
Sea, both sides of the English Channel, both sides of the
Rhine River, both sides of the Atlantic Ocean. Twenty of
them were sitting around the Christmas Tree hearing the
story of Bethlehem, and I said, God Almighty, what kind of
a world will they get? . . . Abraham Lincoln never went to
college but for nine months. We college men, we forget that.
'With firmness in the right as God gives us to see the right.'
. . . If you had that in the United Nations now to determine
what they should do, think what that would mean."

As the spring went on, interest all over America was growing in the answer which MRA offers. It was decided to hold
an Assembly for Moral Re-Armament at Mackinac Island,
in June. The Chairmen and ranking members of the Senate
Foreign Relations and the House of Representatives Foreign
Affairs Committees cabled leaders of many countries about
this conference. They said: "Your presence in the United
States can do much to focus the attention of the American
people on the positive steps that can be taken to answer the
ideological threat of world Communism. We need such a
demonstration of united strength in the field of inspired moral
leadership." [4]

[4] See Document 4, "Inspired Moral Leadership," from Senator Connally
and others; also an invitation to labor leaders from Mr. William Green,
President of American Federation of Labor.

III. TURN ON THE LIGHT

•

"We need a new altitude of living, something above what we have seen as yet," said Frank Buchman in his opening address [5] to the World Assembly for the Moral Re-Armament of the Nations held at Mackinac Island, Michigan, through the first twelve days of June 1951.

Those were twelve days that echoed around the world. One thousand, six hundred and eighty-three delegates from thirty-two countries came to Mackinac. Sixty-four delegates came from seven Far Eastern nations.

Ten special planes from overseas and from within the American continent brought many of the delegates.

The press, radio, television, and film men carried the news to every continent. The Associated Press, one of the world's greatest news-distributing agencies, in a report to its Michigan correspondents stated, "Our coverage of the Moral Re-Armament Assembly at Mackinac Island was the biggest sustained effort of the week. . . . It was evident from the start that newspapers were showing more than usual interest in the gathering."

For at Mackinac a new type of man was molded, a man governed by a fresh range of motives and of aims. Statesmen began to act, no longer just to build up themselves or their own party but to rebuild nations and the world. They began to plan and pattern an inspired democracy that works and that wins.

[5] See Document 5, "Turn on the Light," by Frank N. D. Buchman.

Senator Butler, from Ireland, a land divided against itself as the world today is divided, said, "Idealism is not enough. When men change, they can find unity. There are no horizons to this over-all answer. When I changed and accepted absolute moral standards, I knew it. When I caught the vision of the will of God flowing through the will of men, then suddenly that thing we talk so much about, the will of the people, made sense. It is what we have all been looking for. Inspired democracy is the will of the people accepting the will of God in personal, industrial, national, international affairs—democracy has been given content at last."

Industry began to live at this new altitude. Labor leaders saw that as world renaissance became the accepted aim of the workers, strikes and slowdowns were reactionary methods of settling disputes. While management, taking on the task of remaking the world instead of merely making profits, perceived that exploitation of the workers, inadequate pay, and social injustice were wrong and outmoded.

A chief shop steward of the Transport Workers Union, describing how management had changed, said, "A few months ago production was in the low 60's. Now it is 111%." A superintendent from a big industrial concern said, "The morale of our company is the highest it has ever been. . . . Production is up 25% in some crews." A colored porter declared, "I worked for many years and saw no change in the working conditions of my company. Then MRA came along and the attitude of management has changed." The Chairman of the Shop Stewards of the Dunlop Rubber Company, England, said, "Grievances outstanding for eighteen months were settled and wages raised. Wage increases were given on the basis of labor's co-operation, eliminating restrictive practices in production which have been going on for thirty years."

The class struggle became irrelevant as men of every class were willing to change. Communists learned the secret of changing capitalists, and capitalists, becoming honest about themselves, began to change the communists. One manager of a plant in Europe, who a few months earlier had fought his men bitterly and even struck one of them with his fists, apologized to them. He stood with some of his men on the platform and told how they came to him now to find from him the answer to broken home life which he discovered when he changed.

A docker, a former Communist, who had led many of the most revolutionary strike actions, said, "Moral Re-Armament is an alternative to war. It is the first idea I have found that can stand up to Marxism. MRA brings an end to the class war, and with the end of the class war comes the end of all wars."

The new type of man, learning to take full responsibility for the past as well as the future of his nation, began to emerge at Mackinac. A leader of the Japanese people, one of the delegation of fifty-one who flew from Tokyo to the Assembly, said, "The cause of the present crisis lies in the past and I am also part of the cause. Years ago Japan left the League of Nations, with a proud heart and false confidence that Japan could unite Asia and bring a new order. That began a course of events which led to the present crisis. The Manchurian incident started and then the Chinese incident, and the war in the Pacific came. During these fourteen years the people of Japan have committed many wrongs. And I am very much moved and inspired by experiencing the warm caring of the people who were the enemies of yesterday, forgetting and forgiving our past mistakes. I am compelled to apologize for past wrongs to these people. The need is for everyone in Japan to change according to the four standards of MRA. Now I am burning with the determination to bring back this spirit to Japan and dedicate myself for spreading the idea among my people."

In response to these words a Dutch military man, a former Chief of Staff, stood up and said that three weeks beforehand he would have thought it impossible to forgive the Germans and the Japanese. But in face of what the Japanese leader said he felt ashamed of his hatred and realized that nothing new could be built on hate.

A man from Berlin spoke. His name is Ernst Scharnowski, head of the Trade Unions of Berlin. Berlin today is an island in a Red sea. Those who declare their faith in a free world are marked men. Scharnowski said, "MRA is the only force capable of conquering and curing the creeping paralysis and poison of Communism. Do not regard Berlin as the rearlight of the free world. Regard it as the headlight of freedom illuminating and penetrating the darkness of the East."

The Chairman of the Board of an air line stood on the platform with his wife. They told of a new type of home committed to the reconstruction of a new type of world. The wife said, "We were married twenty-four years ago in France. We had everything. My husband was interested in the air and our home was like a gorgeous airplane. I thought I would enjoy it for the rest of my life. But soon we found we had no radio, no compass, no maps, no charts. We did not know where we were going. So I thought I would take over the controls from the pilot, my husband. Five little passengers, our children, joined us. They all had a rough time. I never asked them where they wanted to go. I took them where I wanted to go. The trips were mostly between the North Pole and the Jungle. We almost crashed many times. Only domination by force, a will that somehow it had to work, kept us airborne. Moral Re-Armament changed everything. It made me realize what a piece of junk our family plane was, when we landed at Mackinac. MRA works. We have maps, compasses, radio. We know where we are going. And we have a Great Pilot. My husband and I just take orders from Him, and our airplane stays on the beam."

The husband said, "I am Chairman of the Board of an airline, but a security analyst from New York by profession. MRA is the best investment by far that I have ever analyzed." He gave point to his words when he announced that he and his wife had decided to give one tenth of their income to the work of Moral Re-Armament in the future. The airlines Chairman added, "We are spending billions of dollars in manufacturing guided missiles. But the world may well be destroyed unless we produce God-guided men as well."

Among the senior military, naval, and air-force officers from many nations who attended the Mackinac Assembly was a great American, Vice-Admiral Morton Deyo.

During World War II, Vice-Admiral Deyo was in command of naval support at Utah Beach, Normandy, the invasion of Cherbourg and the South of France, Iwo Jima, Leyte, and Okinawa. He won the Distinguished Service Medal, the Legion of Merit twice, and other decorations.

He decided two years ago that he would never make another speech or listen to another speech as long as he lived. On his last day at Mackinac he said, "I have listened to speeches here for four or five hours a day and I have sat on the edge of my chair the entire time. Do you know what a cyclotron is? It is an infernal machine which uses about 5,000,000 volts to smash atoms so that scientists will be able to increase the life-span of men. I feel as if I had been an atom in a cyclotron. . . . Here we are in the presence of an answer. The time of this idea has come. . . . Here is a new type of leadership. Frank Buchman's leadership is guided by God, and all are leaders for all are on the same wave length. Here at last is teamwork, with one for all and all for one— and the One is Almighty God."

Another American admiral said: "These people get to the heart and home as no other force I know."

II

Cecil Morrison of Ottawa gave an illustration of the power of MRA to reach through heart and home to the heart of national affairs. Cecil Morrison is a baker. During World

War II he was Bread Administrator for the whole Dominion.

Through MRA, despite a rise in costs of labor and raw materials, he kept the price of bread nationally at a pre-war level. Cecil Morrison told the delegates at Mackinac, "I was born on a farm fifty miles from Ottawa. My people had always been poor and I was determined I was going to be rich. Then I started in the bakery business, with an insatiable ambition to be rich, and I didn't care very much how I got that way.

"At forty I found myself in charge of a chain of bakeries running from Montreal to Victoria, and I thought I had arrived. But then came the depression. In 1932, when I was forty-two, I had lost everything I had, plus thirty thousand dollars I didn't have, plus my position as general manager of this chain of bakeries. Here I was worse off than I was at twenty.

"A strange thing happened that day, the day I lost my last hundred thousand. When I came home I found on my desk an invitation to go to a Moral Re-Armament meeting. So I said to my wife, 'We're broke and this looks to be free, we might as well go.' We went down to the meeting. I listened and I said to my wife, 'This is so simple it may work.'

"I was very much worried about my financial position. I really believed my problem was economic. All I needed was a few thousand dollars, to get started in business again. So I met a chap at this MRA affair and poured out all my financial woes. He said, 'You've sure got a financial problem, but that's not your real problem.' I said, 'Like hell it isn't.' He said, 'Your problem is a moral problem. If you straighten out your moral problem, your financial problem may get right.' I said, 'All right, I'll try it.' He said, 'Are you honest, do you mean business?' I said, 'Yes, I do.' So I prayed. I could only think of one thing to say and that was, 'God, be merciful to me a sinner.' And I meant it. Well, that really changed my life.

"The next thing was to go and be honest with my wife.

There was a big note at the bank which she didn't know about. That was the beginning of a sound home, where in place of my being the dictator we became partners.

"At that time, I used to hate labor leaders like the devil hates Holy Water. At one time in Saskatoon I broke a strike that I could have settled. I was so pig-headed that I won the strike, but I lost a quarter of a million dollars of other people's money.

"MRA had a hard time getting me to see straight on this issue. At one time, the boys in the plant were organizing. I heard about that. One of the men in the plant brought up a briefcase one night and he said, 'Do you want the lowdown on the union?' The night checker had left his briefcase behind. Curiosity got the best of me and I took a peek. My worst fears were realized because I found he had just signed up the night shift. So we had a very sudden reorganization, and I found we could very easily do without this fellow and another one I suspected. The next day I was amazed to find that I had fired the president and secretary of the labor union. It is against the law to interfere with the men organizing, and I got a letter from the Minister of Labor asking for an explanation. I wrote back explaining that business was bad, which satisfied the Department of Labor but didn't satisfy the labor guys.

"Then one morning I woke up about four o'clock and I thought to myself, 'I am really in a jam.' I tried to listen to God. The thought came to me, 'If you want to clean up this mess, start with the briefcase.' I had forgotten all about the briefcase, so I called a caucus of these two men and the labor leaders, and I offered to take them back and apologize. The next day I got a letter from the president of the Canadian Federation of Labor, saying that in thirty years he had never seen an employer put things right like that.

"That made me realize that I needed a new viewpoint on my whole labor policy. From that has developed all the things that we have in our plant, our social welfare program where all the doctors' bills are paid for our employees, life insurance, sick benefits, and pensions. Then we felt that management had a real responsibility for the housing of our workers. So we used the credit of the company to build houses for our people. They now have their own homes, and in twenty years they will own them outright.

"I know that this thing works. All the boys in our bakery are not changed the way I like to think I am. But there are two things that we absolutely agree on. One is that we will put people before things. The other, that all our decisions are based on what is right. When you begin to work those ideas out, things begin to happen."

III

To the Washington Assembly in January 1951, a delegation had come from the West Indies, representing the manufacturers and the unions of Jamaica. They came at a moment of grave crisis. In Jamaica, two rival unions struggle for control of the workers in the rich sugar plantations on which the economic life of the island depends. In December 1950, their struggle reached its climax in a battle to gain control of the famous Worthy Park estate, one of the oldest in Jamaica. The delegation came to Washington in search of an answer. They came back to Mackinac to report the results. In the words of Commander John Edwards, an English planter, they were able to say that "Moral Re-Armament averted a deadlock this year in Jamaica which could have led to civil war."

On the delegation to Mackinac were Mr. Kerr-Jarrett, first Chairman of the Sugar Manufacturers Association of Jamaica, Mr. Kenneth Clarke, the joint owner of the Worthy Park estate over which the struggle had taken place, Mr. Frank Hill, the chief organizer of the trade union which forced the issue at Worthy Park, and the Hon. Wills Isaacs, a leading socialist Member of the House of Representatives. These men are beginning to find a new spirit of unity through Moral Re-Armament.

They spoke from the platform together at Mackinac. Hon. Wills Isaacs described his upbringing in Jamaica, and the pride in Britain which he learned at school. "When we sang 'Rule Britannia' you would have thought we owned a battleship apiece." Then he went to England for the first time and discovered that, although he regarded her as his mother country, she did not regard him as a son, because of his color. "I returned to Jamaica with intense bitterness and hatred for every Englishman. I decided I would never forgive England. We launched the campaign for self-government, and for twelve years I caused more people to hate the English than any other hundred politicians in Jamaica. I became vicious in my attacks on my enemies and gloried in them."

Then he began to meet not only Jamaicans but Englishmen who had begun to change. One was Kerr-Jarrett. Another was Commander Edwards. "Today we are the best friends in the world, and I find an Englishman is not so bad, after all. We are going to work together to bring this new spirit to Jamaica."

On the platform at Mackinac, Wills Isaacs apologized publicly to Kenneth Clarke and his wife for the fact that in the battle at Worthy Park the water-supply line to the Clarke home had been cut for eight weeks, and that they and their children had been kept without water, in the bitterness of the fight.

"Here I have resolved," said Wills Isaacs, "that the Britain I hated so bitterly must be saved at all costs. We cannot save the world unless Britain is saved."

Many thousand miles away in the Far East is another storm center, Malaya, the world's greatest source of rubber, disturbed in the last few years by racial conflict. Two Malayan leaders stood together on the platform at Mackinac, to give the news of the rise of a new spirit in their country which can prove the answer to division and conflict. One of them,

Mrs. Oon, is a member of the Legislative Council of the Federation of Malaya; the other, Thio Chan Bee, is a member of the Legislative and Executive Council of Singapore.

Thio Chan Bee came to the Moral Re-Armament Assembly at Caux, in Switzerland, five years ago. "On my return to Malaya," he said, "I saw that we were on the way to creating civil war. In Malaya we are trying to build a new nation. But I saw that unless we have an ideology that unites, how can we have a new nation?" Thio Chan Bee put all his energies into trying to create a new understanding between the conflicting interests in his country. Many told him he was too late, but he persisted. Finally, The Commissioner General Mr. Malcolm Macdonald was enabled to form the Communities Liaison Committee, which includes leaders of the Malay and Chinese communities. "We have proved that Moral Re-Armament is an ideology which can unite nations," he said. "It can unite the world. The only thing which can prevent this ideology from uniting East and West is if the statesmen and the ordinary man fail to see it and apply it fast enough."

Mrs. Oon added, "If Malaya becomes controlled by subversive elements, what hope is there for South-East Asia? Two years ago I told people in Europe that the attack would come not in Europe but in Asia. There will be many more Koreas, many more ideological attacks. Moral-Re-Armament gives a third way. It shows that West and East can change and unite."

There stood with them the heir to the kingdom of Sarawak, a country as big as New England, with 500,000 inhabitants. His people wanted him to rule over them, but the previous ruler had ceded the country to Britain. There was the risk of widespread bloodshed, and one British governor was assassinated. The heir, listening one night to the Voice of God, felt in his heart the need to build unity in Sarawak at whatever personal cost. He gave up his immediate claims and wrote to his people urging them to unite with the British rather than destroy their heritage with hate.

On the final day of the Assembly, a telegram came from Generalissimo Chiang Kai-shek and Madame Chiang asking the Chinese delegates to lay a wreath on the grave of an American, Bishop Logan Roots, former Primate of China and a pioneer of Moral Re-Armament, who is buried on Mackinac Island. So the men of many nations, former Communists from the Ruhr and the Red Belts of Italy and France, dockworkers from Britain, Japanese, Malayans, industrialists, labor leaders, streamed up the hill and stood by the grave under the bright blue sky and the living green of the forest.

A chorus from many countries sang in memory of Bishop Roots. The Buddhist Abbot, U Rewata, spiritual adviser to the Prime Minister of Burma, who had flown to Mackinac for the Assembly, prayed for the brave men buried on the Island. The Chinese representative, a former Minister of Information, said as he laid a wreath of lilacs, lilies, and roses beneath the great Cross of the grave, "We Chinese have many short-comings. But we do not lack gratitude. And we are grateful to the Bishop and Moral Re-Armament."

Frank Buchman spoke movingly of his old friend. And the leader of a great industry said in amazement, as the races, nations and classes streamed through the sunshine and among the flowers, "I never believed I should see this. It *is* the brotherhood of man. It is staggering. And it all started through the conviction and courage of one man."

Frank Buchman was at the heart of everything throughout these days at Mackinac. He looked personally at every room in the vast hotel which housed the delegates and made sure that each was rightly placed. A newspaperman from Europe, hearing him speak and seeing the sensitive and compelling way in which he handled the sessions of the Assembly, said, "That man bears the imprint of true genius. It is the simplicity of a man's heart with the strength of God inside it." And Frank Buchman fought at Mackinac with the strength of a young man and with a wisdom not his own, that God's will, with its laughter and tears, its freshness and reality, its compassion and its Cross, its power and its healing shall become regnant in the lives of men and nations.

The hotel bellboys and waiters felt part of the Assembly. One of them said, "We have never served such people before." And on the evening when the villagers and their children were invited to meet the delegates, four of the waiters, who had spent their limited off-time rehearsing, sang Negro spirituals as their appreciation for the spirit that had captured the hotel during the Assembly.

A diplomat, a man aware of the pitch of the crisis in the world, said as he left Mackinac, "After this, life can never be the same again for any of us. We have seen miracles in men's lives, illumination in the affairs of states, and new hope for peace."

And Frank Buchman summed up with these words: "My deep personal wish is to have every American free under the direction of God to fight for America; so to fight that America really be free, free from the tyranny of sin, under God's direction—the unseen but ever-present Power. I wish this no less deeply for everyone in every nation. I don't want our sons, especially our fighting sons, to go about without an answer. It simply enslaves them. It is not good enough. It will drive them to the same philosophy that rules our opponents. We shall never create an inspired democracy that way. Men must learn to have a faith that will create the right revolution. If we can spread this revolution fast enough we can save America and the world."

IV. MARXISTS FIND A NEW THINKING

•

What makes a Communist?

One gray day in a gray mining valley the men, as they trudged up the hill between the slagheaps toward the steel works, were singing. They sang because that day their houses were to become their own. Not long before the Company had at last agreed to sell them their homes. Today the final instalments were being handed over.

The men did not know that they were climbing the hill for the last time. That evening they were told that the steel mill was closing. The Company had decided to move the works down to the coast nearer to the ships which brought the iron ore from across the seas.

So the men of the valley were left without hope of employment, while the value of the houses they had bought fell almost to nothing.

If you ask the men and women of that town how their district got its name for revolutionary ardor, that is the story they tell. They learned to hate. They saw no other means of righting their wrongs than through the ideology which Marx and Engels, brooding over the cruel injustices of the industrial West, had brought to birth.

Injustice stirs men to action. When to this is added a philosophy which explains human history in terms of class struggle and asserts the inevitable victory of the oppressed, you see the forging of a force. Ambitious men, bitter men, idealists, intellectuals, men without hope and men with hate add themselves to it for their various reasons. But the strength of

Communism in every land is its hard core of resolute and trained leaders, many of whom have suffered great injustices and who see in Communism their one hope of a better world for themselves and their children.

Can Communists be won to a new thinking and living?

This is the acid test. And it is a significant fact that Communists *are* accepting an ideology more radical in its demands, more satisfying in its life, and more certain in its promise of a new world than the ideology of Marx. This is the ideology of Moral Re-Armament. Men of iron from the very furnace of European Communism, from the Ruhr and the Rhondda, the Red Belt of Paris and industrial Lombardy, Party members of twenty years' standing, they are turning to MRA in growing numbers. And they fight for it with the vigor and resource of trained revolutionaries.

I

What makes a Communist change?

For nearly a century the Ruhr, the industrial heart of Europe, has had steady Marxist indoctrination.

Here the gulf between wealth and poverty has been wide. Bitterness is deep and violent. Many of the workers in the Ruhr are trained shock-troopers in ideological warfare.

Between 1948 and 1950 there were hundreds of meetings on Moral Re-Armament in factories and trade union branches as well as in the provincial Parliaments of Western Germany. Millions have read about it in the newspapers or heard of it in frequent radio programs; 140,000 workers, trade union officials, industrial and political leaders have seen Moral Re-Armament plays in twenty-four cities.

One cold winter night a veteran Communist leader, Max Bladeck, took the chair at one of these trade union meetings. Bladeck is head of the works council of one of the largest collieries in the Ruhr. He is a small man, every inch a fighter, with sharp eyes, an intellectual forehead, and a chest racked by silicosis. He has been for twenty-five years a member of the Communist Party. The meeting was in a beer hall.

When the Moral Re-Armament men arrived, amid the smoke and the glasses and the lights, they found that Bladeck had arranged for some of the most skillful Communist speakers in his district to address and demolish them.

Six Communists spoke one after the other. They went on the attack. They spoke for an hour on the theme that in the heart of every capitalist is a Fascist and that Western nations are preparing the next world war. They quoted Marx on the need to change the system, and Stalin's dictum that the bourgeois had never yet put principle before profit. Pointing to the history of the churches, they declared that Christianity had tried for two thousand years to build a new world—and failed. Now it was their turn.

At this point the MRA men took the floor. One of their spokesmen, a worker from Lancashire, began by admitting that his own country, Britain, had sometimes made mistakes. The Germans acted as if they had never heard such a thing said by an Englishman before. Their interest was caught.

"Everybody," added this man, "wants to see the other fellow change. Every nation wants to see the other nation change. Yet everybody is waiting for the other fellow to begin." They were listening now, and there were cries of "Hear! Hear!" all over the hall.

"*But*," the spokesman continued, "the best place to start is with yourself. Why not start with our own class, our own race, our own nation, and then carry it to the world?"

Other speakers dealt with changing the system. "Every decent man hates the social injustice and economic misery of the world," one of them said. "There is enough in the world for everyone's need but not for everyone's greed. If everybody cared enough and everybody shared enough, wouldn't everybody have enough? Just changing the system does not go far enough. Christians have often failed to live what they talk about, but the idea may still be right. Moral Re-Armament stands for the *full* dimension of change—social change, economic change, national change, international change, all based on personal change. Anything less is reactionary."

Then, through the smoky air, amid tense silence a shipyard worker from Clydeside declared: "Labour has never been so powerful and never been so divided. We have learned to split the atom. But we have not learned to unite humanity. The Labour movement has within it the seeds of its own defeat— unless it learns to change human nature. Human nature *can* be changed. It must be changed on a colossal scale—capitalists, Americans, British, yes, even Communists and Germans—all over the world. Then the classless society will appear. We won't have to wait for it till we are in our graves."

A Canadian industrialist was introduced. His changed attitude toward labor amazed the Communists. The meeting lasted for four hours. Not a man had left the hall.

Battles like this were fought daily in the Ruhr. Many questions were asked and answered. Week after week for months on end the MRA men met the miners in their homes and in the pits. As a result hundreds of workers and their leaders went to Caux in Switzerland, the permanent headquarters of MRA, where a World Assembly for Moral Re-Armament was in session. Among them were Bladeck and another veteran Communist, Paul Kurowski.

At Caux these men saw a living demonstration of an ideology based on change, change not for one class but for every class. "For twenty-five years I have sung the *Internationale* with all my heart and strength," said Kurowski, after some days there, "but this is the first time I have seen it lived."

They began to change. But change is never comfortable, whether for a Communist, a capitalist, or anyone else. It means facing absolute moral standards. It will involve being different at home. It may call for a break with personal habits or long-cherished points of view.

Bladeck and Kurowski talked far into the night with each other and with the Moral Re-Armament men. They fought back with every club in the Marxist bag. But always they were held by the affection of their new friends and by the relentless logic of the MRA ideology.

Finally Kurowski stated their conclusion: "Anyone who will not follow the absolute standards of honesty, purity, unselfishness, and love is a traitor to his class and to his nation."

Kurowski, whom thirteen years under Hitler had not shaken from his Communist allegiance, began to reassess Marxism in the light of the evidence of Caux. "I am beginning to see that the basic theories of Marxism are out of date," he said. "Its philosophy is built on German classical philosophy and fails to reckon with the important fact that human nature can be changed. Its economic theory is equally out of date, as we have attained many of the things for which the workers were then striving and have now moved on from the industrial to the ideological age. Its tactic of class war is suicide, for it is bound to end in universal war between two groups and therefore lead to world destruction." [7]

Meanwhile, back in the Ruhr, reports were received by the West German Communist Party that Bladeck and Kurowski were beginning to accept the ideology of Moral Re-Armament. The Party became alarmed. They sent one of their most trusted members, Willi Benedens, to get arguments against Bladeck, Kurowski, and MRA.

Benedens was a district political secretary of the Communist Party. He had been elected chairman for a Ruhr district of the proposed communist Socialist Unity Party—and it was on his initiative that Molotov protested when the Western Powers suppressed that party. Benedens had been removed from Hitler's air force because his convictions became suspect and had been transferred to the infantry, where he lost both legs.

What happened when he came to Caux? It can best be described in his own words. "I fought bitterly against my friends who went to Caux and who were officials of the Com-

[7] See Document 7, "A Communist's Ten Points."

munist Party," said Benedens. "But when I came there I found the thing I had for years fought for—the classless society. I found there an ideology which led to social justice and satisfied the needs of the human heart. It is an idea that can solve the social problems of the West and lead to a solution between East and West, since Moral Re-Armament is not *against* but *for* something. It is *for* change in everyone everywhere in the world."

Willi Benedens backed his convictions by change in his own life, which is the hallmark of an effective ideological fighter. "I saw I had to change completely," said Benedens. "First, within my family, then in my relations with my neighbors and my colleagues in the mines. I was a great speaker about peace, but I could not get along with my fellow shop-stewards. At Caux I found a bridge from myself to my fellow men. Change is a platform on which people of all nations can find the way to each other."

Benedens, Kurowski, and Bladeck returned to the Ruhr together. They were called before the Communist Party Executive. They gave a simple explanation. "We have found," they said, "an ideology greater than Communism."

The West German Communist Party was in a dilemma. For years the Leninist strategy has been for Communism to infiltrate into the structure of society and change it. Yet here were men, not weaklings but the hard core of the Party, who went to Caux and themselves were changed.

Meanwhile, the three men had called a meeting of the Party stalwarts. In a description of this meeting they wrote, "The going was hot. But the longest speech has to stop some time. Ten men can sing together, but they cannot talk together. When ten men talk at once, you cannot tell what anyone is saying. When we spoke of Caux the loud voices became quieter. Soon they were all listening, silent and thoughtful. Our chairman is already so far advanced that you might think he had been at Caux himself."

In a formal letter to the Executive, Bladeck, Kurowski, and

Benedens recommended that the Party make itself conversant with "the world-revolutionizing new idea" of Moral Re-Armament, quoted Marx and Engels to justify their course, stated that they had decided to change themselves "on reasonable and realistic grounds," and announced that they "already had changed many other Communists."

According to one of the members, after a heated Party caucus, "At the end of two hours you would have thought that Moral Re-Armament was the only thing Marx had ever fought for, and that Moscow and everyone else up till now had never really understood him."

The official Communist newspaper in Western Germany, *Freies Volk*, on October 6, 1949, came out with a major article written by the chairman of the Ruhr regional committee of the Party, Hugo Paul, on Moral Re-Armament. It said: "The dangerous activity of Moral Re-Armament has been underestimated by the District Executive and by the Regional Executive of the Party and has led to ideological uncertainties in sections of the Party. . . . These men from Caux have been recommending that the Party make itself conversant with the world-revolutionizing new ideas of Moral Re-Armament."

The men from Caux stood firm. From Essen, Dortmund, and other parts of the Ruhr seasoned Marxists joined them in their fight. One of the founders of the powerful Steele-Essen Communist Party, Hermann Stoffmehl, the Town Clerk of Alten-Essen, announced that he now believed MRA was the uniting ideology needed by the world. If the Communist Party would not accept it, he would not only leave the Party himself but a third of the local membership would go with him.

Finally, the West German Communist Party removed forty regional leaders of the Party, including Hugo Paul, who had written the article on MRA, for having "dealings with a contrary ideology." "Moral Re-Armament aims at the re-education of the human being and the reconciliation of the classes," said the Party's explanation, "and therefore must confuse fighters for class war."

The Executive of the Communist Party of Western Germany was summoned on January 8, 1950, to a special conference in Düsseldorf at which they stated they were going to reorganize the entire Executive and Secretariat because it had been "tainted with an ideology inimical to the Party."

The *Manchester Guardian* on February 8, 1950, under the heading "A New Communist Heresy—Moral Re-Armament," quoted the new Communist Party Chairman in the Ruhr, Herr Ledwohn, in referring to the recent purge of the entire executive body, as stating, "one of the most dangerous symptoms was the growing connections between Party members and the Moral Re-Armament movement."

Meanwhile, Bladeck, Kurowski and Benedens, the originators of this revolution, had won re-election to their works councils with increased majorities in the face of bitter attack.

II

Eight-year-old boys going down into the darkness of the mines to work twelve-hour shifts—the military were occupying the mining valleys during strikes and lockouts—more than half of the population of South Wales unemployed for years on end—colliery owners making millions out of the industry to invest more profitably outside Wales. These are some of the memories which have embittered the South Wales mining valleys and have transformed them into a spearhead of the British revolutionary movement.

A Moral Re-Armament task force took its industrial play, *The Forgotten Factor*,[6] to the Welsh valleys. In six weeks thirty-five thousand people saw it. Ideologically alive, they were swift to grasp its significance. "Greater than Marx," said the *South Wales Argus* later. "An ideology stronger than

[6] See Document 6, "*The Forgotten Factor*," addresses at World première by Senator Harry S. Truman and Representative James W. Wadsworth.

Marxism," commented the *Aberdare Leader*, one of the most trusted of the valley papers.

Men began to change in the mines and steelworks. Typical is the story of Jack Jones, a steelworker who for twenty-eight years had followed the Communist line. He had trained his daughter until she had become even more radical than himself. He started as a miner and lost the sight of an eye in the pits. He was unemployed for thirteen years. "I sacrificed everything in the class struggle," says Jack, "my home, my comfort, the love of my wife—I even sacrificed my daughter on the altar of Marxism."

Jones was elected Union branch representative in his department of the Ebbw Vale steelworks, one of the largest steel strip mills in Europe. He went to negotiate with the manager, who had the reputation of being a dictator. But unknown to Jones the manager had previously met MRA. His whole attitude to life had altered.

"When I went into that man's office, a man I hated, a man I distrusted, a man who represented the devil to me, I was faced by a man with a superior ideology," says Jones. "He spoke about absolute honesty and what was right. He told me how his own attitude to the workers had had to alter. I thought he was a crook. I went home and told my wife I had met someone who had gone nuts. 'Why don't you take a look at yourself in the mirror?' she said to me, 'You're no Michelangelo.' Then she said, 'You always criticize everybody else. What about yourself?' I stayed awake at night thinking.

"Then I went and told the manager, 'I will try and work this out with you.' But at first I had my hands in my pockets for fear he would try to pick them. Yet the spirit we built together has lasted."

Jones is a new man and his family is a new family. He and his manager have traveled together in Europe, America, and all over Britain to show what can happen when a worker who has spent twenty-eight militant years proclaiming his belief in the theories of Karl Marx meets a man with a superior ideology.

Moral Re-Armament spread swiftly through the Welsh valleys. Another Jack Jones, the miner novelist, justly called "The Voice of Wales," sums it up this way: "Something far more revolutionary than Communism has hit the Rhondda Valley. Moral Re-Armament has started a revolution in the spirit of the community. . . . People have welcomed Moral Re-Armament as their deliverance from the tyranny of the 'isms' which have for so long directed them to roads leading nowhere."

Facts prove the change that has taken place in the thinking of the valleys. For example, Harry Pollitt, the General Secretary of the Communist Party of Great Britain, fighting in Rhondda East in 1945, polled 15,761 votes. In 1950, he polled only 4,463. The voting for the Rhondda Urban District Council shows the same trend. There is now no Communist member on the Council.

III

Italy is one of the most explosive situations in Western Europe. Two million are unemployed, while millions more work only half the week because of overpopulation and the shortage of raw materials. Wages are low—it is rare for a family to be able to exist on the wages of one breadwinner—while a few live in great luxury. There is practically no middle class. Italy has the largest Communist Party in Europe outside Russia.

Five hundred workers—one hundred of them Communists— came from the industrial North of Italy to the Caux Assembly in 1950. They came in parties of fifty, often with some of the management from their plants.

When one of the management-labor delegations from the Montecatini Industries returned to Milan, an executive apologized to the Communist works-council chairman for the bitterness with which they had fought. Eighty per cent of the men in this factory are Communist. But within a week it was decided by a unanimous vote of the workers to take down the portrait of Stalin in the canteen and replace it by a picture of Christ on the Cross. At the same time it was decided that office staff and factory workers would in future eat together in one canteen.

One of the company officials at this plant was so unpopular that, a few months before his coming to Caux, the men, downing their tools, refused to let him enter the plant. This man says, "I was convinced the only way to hold my authority over them was by force. I treated them brutally." At Caux he changed. He became honest with his workers. They began to come to this company official with their troubles. One of them told him in confidence how the money which should go to his wife and three children was being spent on another woman. The company official helped him to be honest with his wife and to break off the wrong relationship. Now, every time they meet, the worker thanks the official, whom he used to hate, for having helped him to remake his home. A new spirit is spreading all through the plant.

One of the leading Communists from the Milan area, head of a factory works council, came with two of the works-council members. After his first evening at Caux he said, "This is reality." After a few days he said, "We have not always been honest in what we have told the masses." He decided to measure his own life against the absolute moral standards of honesty, purity, unselfishness, and love. He spent that evening talking things over with the director of personnel in his factory, a man whom he had regarded as his greatest enemy. All night long he did not sleep. Early in the morning he went to see another member of the works council, a man of opposite political views, and was honest about himself and his motives. On leaving Caux he said that he was in touch with fifty thousand Communists in cells around Milan, and added, "I will fight for MRA when I get back." On his return he was called in by the Communist Party and asked to explain why he had disobeyed Party orders. He was immediately expelled, but his response was to send some of his friends to Caux. They reported that his change had become the main topic of conversation in the local cafés.

The Communist-controlled Chamber of Labor in Milan attacked Moral Re-Armament and the visits to Caux. In spite of this warning, widely publicized in the Communist press, the next delegation from Italy was forty per cent Communist. They came from the largest steel works of Italy, situated in an area known as Little Stalingrad. Here at the end of the war a director was thrown alive into the furnaces and two others were shot. A present director says that on one occasion when the workers came to see him in his office they didn't beat the table, they beat him. One of these workers was with him at Caux, and apologized to him there.

After the return of the first group of these steelworkers to Italy, one Communist said, "It was like a bomb exploding." Two of them, described as the "most intelligent members of the works council," said, "If the Communist Party will not accept the principles of Moral Re-Armament, we shall leave the Communist Party." Another Communist said, "If I had been here four years ago my wife would not have left me. I am no longer led by the Kremlin. I am a man from Caux."

IV

A French Communist sat down at Caux with two senior officers. He spoke bluntly but quietly: "You talk of national defense. But what have the workers of France, who will be the soldiers under your command, to defend? At the present time the French worker has nothing to defend. His standard of living can scarcely fall any lower. What has he to lose? Unless you can give the workers of France an adequate life, free from exploitation, which is worth fighting for, they will flock to the first program which offers them immediate returns. There are only two real choices before the workers of France today. One is the revolution of Communism; and the other is the revolution of Moral Re-Armament."

The Communist, Robert Leblond, had come from Paris with his colleague, Gérard Fourmond. They work in the Poissy factory, which makes sixty per cent of the universal joints for the French automobile industry. The factory is opposite the great Ford works.

During the last major strike in that area, Fourmond was particularly in demand. He had invented a new type of nail which, when thrown on the ground, would always fall point upward. These were spread liberally on the roads outside the Ford factory to damage the police cars. When Fourmond decided to apply MRA, one of the first things he did was to tell his employer that he had been making the nails from the company's material on the company's time. Fourmond and Leblond are two of many French Communists who have taken up the fight for Moral Re-Armament.

In the industrial North, twenty thousand workers have seen *The Forgotten Factor* played by a French cast. At a ten-day assembly at Le Touquet workers and employers came together at the height of the 1948 coal strike, which is said to have deprived France of coal equivalent in value to six months' Marshall Aid. Forty-five groups of workers came from various factories and mines, including many from the CGT unions leading the strike. A director of the French National Coal Board, stated that the move back to work was given its initial impetus by miners' leaders fresh from the Le Touquet assembly.

Another of the Marxists who has taken up the fight in France is Roger Braquier of Mantes, near Paris. Abandoned at birth by his father and drifting apart from his mother, he was seldom far from starvation through his childhood, often sleeping under bridges and searching in garbage cans for his food. "When I discovered Marxism," he says, "it became for me a burning passion and I wanted to destroy, destroy—always destroy—to make a new world possible. But I have now found that Moral Re-Armament goes further than Marxism, and for one very simple reason. While fighting as before for the happiness and a means of livelihood for others, it has permitted me and my family to know happiness ourselves. For fifteen years my wife and child have been set aside for the class struggle. It's a hard thing for a woman to marry a rebel. But now my wife says: 'Roger, our family has found unity. I'm going to go with you, even if it means leaving my boy behind for a time. Because to fight for a better world together is the best way we can express our love for him.' Actually we do it all three together."

When Roger came home from his first meeting with MRA his little son ran to his mother with tears of joy and said, "Is Dad always going to stay like this?"

v

Hans Bjerkholt, a founder of the Communist Party in Norway in 1923, and ever since then a member of the national executive, came to Caux. Previously he had three times visited Moscow as a delegate to the Comintern.

Since 1936 he has been a full-time official of the Trade Unions of Norway and is the Secretary of the Trades Council from Östfold. After some days at Caux he declared, "Is there a way out? I believe there is. I have seen here that human beings can be changed. I believe we can find an ideology which unites everyone above class, above race. . . . If I can change, anyone in my party can change. It is a hard and heavy work we have before us. But no difficulties can prevent me from doing what I know to be right."

Bjerkholt returned to his country. Early in 1951, following his resignation from the Communist Party, he issued this statement to the press:

"My resignation from the Norwegian Communist Party results from my recognition of an adherence to Moral Re-Armament, and still further to the consequences which follow therefrom.

"The Party received my view on these questions some time ago in a full written statement.

"Of course, I could not expect that the Norwegian Communist Party would accept right away as its working basis the (in my view) revolutionary policy which Moral Re-Armament represents, but I have always in politics and thinking, openly and without any digression, maintained fully my conviction. This I will continue to do.

"After serious and thorough consideration of all the existing problems I have come to the conclusion that the only logical and valid solution is to bring my membership of the Norwegian Communist Party to an end.

"It is, however, my hope that in our country also many Communists, socialists, progressive and unprejudiced people generally will turn out pioneers in the fight for this new thinking which mankind and our own common future depend on."

Since that time Bjerkholt has fought in the trade union movement, over the radio, and at mass meetings in his own and other countries to carry this new thinking to the world.

VI

Western governments are no longer inclined, as they once were, to underestimate the power of the long arm of world Communism, stretching far beyond the most advanced Russian military outpost. Driven into a fever of activity to make up for the years of ideological somnolence, they set up new government departments, allocate millions, build wireless stations, expel Communists from office, and outlaw Communist Parties.

Yet it becomes plainer every day that world unity cannot be created merely by fulminating against Communism. Anyone who has traveled in Asia, Germany, France, or Italy knows that. It is equally certain that Moral Re-Armament has been making inroads in the very areas where Western governmental propaganda is at a discount. The reasons are not hard to find. MRA has no axe to grind. It stands four-square for change in Communists and anti-Communists alike. And it advances through the impetus of people who are practicing what they preach.

Where will all this lead? Does it mark the turning of the tide? Certainly in Germany the Communists have already circulated instructions forbidding Party members to attend MRA gatherings or to fraternize with its leaders.*

Their orders closely parallel the directives from Gestapo headquarters warning Nazi officials against MRA before and during the war.[8] For it is a curious, thought-provoking fact that both the Communist and Nazi hierarchy have put a higher rating on MRA's world-wide activity than have many in the democracies. Both have honored it with serious and relentless opposition.

Yet MRA's leadership refuses today to join in the topical tirades against Communism, just as before the war they refused to add to the spate of anti-Nazi rhetoric. MRA's approach to the Communists is not to outlaw them, but to outmode them. It fights for change as they do, but for change not just in one class but in every class and every person.

Communists are rising to this new level of thinking. The stories in this chapter, from Germany, Britain, France, Norway and Italy, could be multiplied many times both from within these countries and elsewhere. They are part of a ferment of new thinking and living in many lands, a phenomenon which embraces Marxists from India and Japan, the Americas and Australasia, the docks of Rotterdam and the ore mines of Northern Sweden.

This is what Frank Buchman, the initiator of Moral Re-Armament, had in mind when he said, in May 1950, "Marx-

---

* Hubert Stein, a member of the Executive Committee of the German National Union of Mine Workers, stated in June 1951: "In the last three years the number of communists on the Works Councils of the Ruhr has dropped from 72% to 25%. The main credit must go to MRA."

[8] See Document 8, "The Gestapo Report."

ists are finding a new thinking in a day of crisis. The class struggle is being superseded. Management and labor are beginning to live the positive alternative to class war.

"Can you imagine Marxists so different that their employers say of them, 'They are our best friends'? Can you imagine an industrialist so different that the workers ask to see his passport before they will believe the miracle of his change? These things are true. They are happening. They are the one hope of finding unity for all. Is there any difference between West and East when this becomes a fact?

"Is change for all the one basis of unity for all? Can Marxists be changed? Can they have this new thinking? Can Marxists pave the way for a greater ideology? Why not? They have always been open to new things. They have been forerunners. They will go to prison for their belief. They will die for their belief. Why should they not be the ones to live for this superior thinking?"

V. ROAD TO A NEW EUROPE

•

Europe is torn not only by the class war within nations but by the hates and hurts that linger from the wars between the nations.

Paper pacts, grudging concessions, and interminable conferences do not heal these wounds. No answer is complete today unless it can solve such problems as the centuries-old fear and bitterness between nations like France and Germany.

For example, statesmen have been perplexed about how to fit both these countries into a European defense system.

Strong forces of opinion in France opposed giving arms to Germans, though the military experts insisted that German manpower would be invaluable in European defense. France, having been so often invaded, was afraid of Germany.

On the other hand, many Western Germans were loath to be armed as infantrymen and bear the brunt of any attack from the East, while the French and other Allied forces would be able to retreat toward prepared positions nearer the Channel.

But consider the Eastern section of Germany. Russia, like France, was invaded by Germany. Yet the Russians did not hesitate to arm the Germans in the East. They were not afraid of having the Germans once more turn upon them, because they had been imbuing masses of young Germans with a new ideology. These young men were ready to be trained as soldiers. They had been given something to fight for.

Once again the ideological factor emerged as decisive, and a crucial point in the defense of the free world becomes, "How can France and Germany find a purpose big enough to lift them above the hatred of the years?"

But quite apart from issues of defense, the world knows that there can be no European unity unless the Germans and the French find some new way of living together. Mr. Churchill stated the need. The question remained, "Who will provide the answer?"

I

On June 4, 1950, a unique event took place at Gelsenkirchen in the heart of the Ruhr. This is the area where eighty-six per cent of German heavy industry is found, and where furnaces and mines have provided massive strength for Germany in three major wars. Here, in the presence of a group of distinguished Germans, a Senator of France, Mme. Eugénie Eboué, on behalf of her nation, presented the scarlet ribbon and Cross of Chevalier of the Legion of Honor to Frank Buchman. She said, "This is a symbol of the new friendship between the French and the German people." A telegram of congratulation came from leaders of the French Government.*

A British estimate of this "new friendship between France and Germany" is worth recording. It comes from Major-General S. W. Kirby, who was Deputy Chief of Staff to the Control Commission in Germany. Speaking of the work of Moral Re-Armament he says, "Progress has already been sufficiently rapid to have altered in several respects the relationship between Germany and France on the highest levels, and from all reports it would appear that in the spread of this ideology and in its taking root within the Western nations the great hope for the future lies."

II

And what is the story behind all this? When the last war ended and the Russian, American, French, and British forces

---

* The telegram was signed by Paul Bacon, Minister of Labor; Claudius Petit, Minister of Reconstruction; Robert Prigent, Minister of State in the President's Council; by five former Cabinet Ministers; by two Vice-Presidents of the National Assembly; by the President of the Commission of the Interior; by the President of the Commission of Labor; and by ten Members of the Chamber of Deputies.

had seized the body of Germany, many people began to talk
about the "ideological vacuum." They feared that either
Communism or a new form of fanatical nationalism would
arise in Germany unless this "ideological vacuum" left in the
hearts of millions were filled. But filled by what?

In 1947 some men from Caux went to see General Lucius
Clay, who at that time was running affairs for America in
Germany. They explained that the purpose of Caux was to
train men to rebuild their nations on sound moral foundations.
They suggested that the leadership of Germany, which until
that moment had not been able to leave their country, might
come to Caux to receive this training.

It was with the assistaance of General Clay, as well as of
Lord Pakenham, at that time the minister responsible to the
British Cabinet for German affairs, that one hundred and
fifty picked German leaders came to Caux that year.

Karl Arnold, Prime Minister of North Rhine-Westphalia,
says of this invitation, "We are indebted to Moral Re-Armament because after World War II it was the first to enter into
talks with us in an atmosphere free from any humiliating distrust. . . . We have taken a wrong way to its logical end.
Now we have a great opportunity. We can begin to take
an entirely new way. . . . In our Cabinet we have already
begun to see the fruits of this ideology at work. When the
nations of the world seek the good road with conviction and
passion, then I believe there is a new beginning for the
world."

The hundred and fifty German leaders who came to Caux
in 1947 decided their nation must have a handbook setting out
their new philosophy. It was called *Es Muss Alles Anders
Werden*, "Everything must be different."

There was no paper, no money, no labor. But Swedes who
had been to Caux organized a gift of one hundred tons of
paper. In Germany, at a time when electricity often failed
and the cold was so intense that the ink sometimes froze in
the machines, volunteers worked day and night. One million

copies of this handbook were printed; thousands of them found their way behind the Iron Curtain.

Next year, 1948, 450 Germans, leaders from different walks of life, came to Caux.* Dr. Konrad Adenauer, West German Federal Chancellor, was there. Nine of his family have also attended as have several members of his Cabinet.

Many of the German leaders who came to Caux in 1948 insisted that Caux should come to Germany. So on October 9, 1948, the largest civilian cavalcade to visit Germany since the war rolled over the Swiss frontier at Schaffhausen. Two hundred and sixty people from thirty nations took the revue, *The Good Road*, which presents inspired democracy with drama, music, and pageant, through Munich, Stuttgart, Frankfurt, Düsseldorf, and Essen.

In the space of three weeks, twenty thousand Germans saw the show. Thousands more who could not get into the theater talked with the cast for hours in the streets or cafés of the cities.

The London *News Chronicle* quoted a Military Government official as saying, "Moral Re-Armament has done more to win the German people to democracy in three weeks than we have done in three years."

In November 1948, at the insistence of Karl Arnold's Cabinet, an international task force set to work in the Ruhr. Their main weapon was *The Forgotten Factor* in German.

Its première was given in Essen in a theater which stands

---

* Among other German leaders who have been to Caux are: Minister Presidents Karl Arnold of North Rhine-Westphalia, Reinhold Maier of Würtemberg-Baden, Hans Ehard of Bavaria and Gebhardt Müller of Würtemberg-Hohenzollern; Federal Ministers Gustav Heinemann (Interior until his resignation in October 1950), Hans Lukaschek (Refugees), Anton Storch (Labor), Eberhard Wildermuth (Housing); trade unionists, Dr. Hans Böckler (Chairman of the Trade Union Congress), Mr. Karl Goroncy (Treasurer, National Union of Mineworkers), Mr. Ernst Scharnowski (President of the Trade Unions of Western Berlin); industrialists Dr. Otto Springorum (General Manager, Gelsenkirchen Coal Mining Company); Dr. Theo Goldschmidt (President, Goldschmidt Chemical Company); Martin Schwab (Chairman, Telefunken, Stuttgart); Mr. Fritz Hardach (Commercial Director, Krupps).

stark and bare amid the shambles of what was once the mighty Krupp Armament Works.

That was the start of a tour during which 120,000 Germans, mostly miners and their families, saw *The Forgotten Factor*.[9] *Die Bergbau Industrie*, official organ of the Ruhr's five hundred thousand miners, headlined their account: "MRA—A New Dimension."

Spokesmen from the Moral Re-Armament force addressed the Socialist Party caucus in seven West German Parliaments. They spoke to more than two hundred trade union meetings where the audiences were usually ninety per cent Marxist.

They were invited to Berlin. An international delegation was flown in at the time of the airlift. They were received by the Lord Mayor, Professor Ernst Reuter, addressed Members of Parliament and consulted with the Chairman of the Berlin Social Democrat Party, Franz Neumann, and members of his executive as well as with Ernst Scharnowski, head of the Berlin Trade Unions.

The Berlin Socialist daily, *Telegraf*, commented, "Here is an army of people whose principles go to the root of the political, economic, national, and social problems with astonishing clarity."

With the rising tide of interest twenty-six hundred of the leadership of Germany were among the delegates who came to Caux in 1949 and 1950.

III

Germans who are won by the ideology of Moral Re-Armament are ready to admit the guilt of their nation and their share in it. This change of heart is not mere words. It convinces those who could be expected to be most skeptical.

Take a typical instance—Peter Petersen of Hamburg. At the age of eight he was enlisted by the Nazis. Later he was selected to attend a special training school for future leaders of the Third Reich, and served in the crack Gross Deutschland

[9] See Document 9, "Millions Ready."

Division. When the war was over he was jailed by the British. In his own words, "I thought our enemies had better weapons in war. But that was no reason for me to change my ideology. Because I was careless enough to say that to other people I was put in prison by the British. When I came out of prison I was more careful, but had not changed my mind at all."

Petersen talked with some of the MRA people in Germany and came to Caux. After some time there he said, "I was trained from boyhood in a false ideology. Even my country's collapse could not shake my beliefs. But MRA did. I saw where I was wrong when they showed me what was right.

"I felt I had to change, not just as Peter Petersen, but as a German. I had to identify myself completely with Germany, though previously I had tried again and again to excuse myself. I saw that no real new beginning could come just by forgetting, but only by forgiveness."

Communists from the Ruhr who suffered under Hitler have met Petersen and others like him, talked with them, and worked with them for weeks at a stretch. They say frankly that if they had had the secret of changing youth like Petersen as he and his friends have now been changed, Hitler might never have come to power in Germany.

One Frenchwoman whom Peter Petersen heard speak at Caux and who has played a great part in building a bridge between the French and the German people is Mme. Irène Laure. For many years she has been a leading figure in the French Socialist movement, a member of the Executive of the Party, Member of Parliament for Marseilles, her home town, and was head of the Socialist women of her country.

She is a nurse by profession. Her husband is a merchant seaman, for forty-seven years a Marxist, trained by Marcel Cachin, the veteran French Communist.

She is a quiet, gray figure, almost insignificant until she speaks. Then her voice carries the certainty of conviction born from experience.

She was a key figure in the resistance movement in France

during the war. She was one of those who concealed the French sailors from the Nazis after the scuttling of the French fleet at Toulon.

When the German authorities in Marseilles attempted to put pressure on the people by cutting down their food, and all the male authorities of the city were too scared to intervene, she organized a host of Marseilles women, gave them orders for silence, and marched them like angels of vengeance through the city streets to confront the Nazi authorities. The rations were restored.

The Gestapo took her son and tortured him. She came out of the war dominated by one thing—her hatred of Germany.

"I had only one wish," she says. "To destroy them all."

She was invited to Caux. She went with skepticism but thinking that it would be a nice holiday for herself and her son. On her first day there she heard some Germans addressing the Assembly. But these Germans were saying things that Mme. Laure had never heard Germans say before. They were honestly facing the mistakes of the past and their own nation's need of change.

The Frenchwoman's heart was full of hate and wonder, fear and hope, doubt and belief. For three weeks she fought, as she says, "to find a flea in the straw" somewhere at Caux. But she, with more reason than most to distrust Germans, was convinced that the change she had seen was real and would last.

She faced the fact that her hatred of Germany was helping to divide Europe; that her hatred of another class was helping to divide France; that her dislike of some of her own party was helping to divide the Socialist movement. It was an intense struggle. But the day came when she stood on the platform and asked forgiveness of the Germans.

Six months later she and her husband left their home to travel with the force of Moral Re-Armament through Germany. With them was one young Frenchman who had lost fifteen members of his family in Hitler's gas chambers, and another, a man, of whose family twenty-two had been sent to concentration camps, never to come out again.

The Laures lived in the homes of the Germans and spoke to millions on the radio and at mass meetings. They spoke in seven of the Parliaments of the West German states.

Irène Laure says, "Can you think what it meant in change for me to go to Germany? In my heart I had willed the ruins that I saw there. I am a mother and a grandmother, I am a Socialist and all my life have talked about fraternity, yet I had longed for those ruins. I had to ask forgiveness for my hatred from those people who were living in the ruins. I had to ask forgiveness from those fifty thousand women whom I saw gray with fatigue, clearing the rubble in Berlin, and who the Lord Mayor told us would take thirty years at their present rate of progress to finish the task.

"I do not forget the ruins in my own or in other countries that the Germans invaded. Not at all. But the thing I could do was to face my own hatred and ask forgiveness for it. Change in me brought forth change in many Germans. Moral Re-Armament is the greatest force that has created unity between our two nations. A common ideology is doing for France and Germany today what sentimentality never did between the two wars."

IV

This spirit has begun to sweep through France. It has begun to take a real hold in areas like the industrial North. In a speech made in September 1950, M. Pleven, the Prime Minister, stated, "The moral re-armament of France is essential."

Three subjects are on the agenda of the French Institute of National Defense, which is under his control:

(1) European Unity.
(2) The German question.
(3) Moral re-armament of the French nation.

The ideology of Moral Re-Armament is very near to the heart and hopes of M. Robert Schuman, the French Foreign Minister. M. Schuman is a friend of Frank Buchman. He contributed the foreword to the French edition of Frank Buchman's speeches, *Refaire le Monde*, published in 1950. In this foreword [10] M. Schuman said, "Moral Re-Armament brings us a philosophy of life applied in action. . . . It is not a question of a change of policy; it is a question of changing men. Democracy and her freedoms can be saved only by the quality of the men who speak in her name. That is what Dr. Buchman expresses in simple and moving words. He has declared war on materialism and individualism, twin generators of our selfish divisions and social injustices. May he be heard and followed more and more in all nations of the world by those who today still clash in fratricidal hatred."

Frank Buchman is also the friend of Dr. Konrad Adenauer. Dr. Adenauer summarized his own evaluation of the effect of Moral Re-Armament in a message he sent to Frank Buchman in June 1951. He said: "It is my conviction, too, that men and nations cannot outwardly enjoy stable relationships until they have been inwardly prepared for them. In this respect Moral Re-Armament has rendered great and lasting services. The German people gratefully recognizes the help which has so readily come to them through Moral Re-Armament. In Western Germany, Moral Re-Armament has worked very forcefully in the creation of good relations between management and labor. In recent months, too, we have seen the conclusion, after some difficult negotiations, of important international agreements. Here, also, I believe, Moral Re-Armament has played an unseen but effective part in bridging differences of opinion between the negotiating parties, and has kept before them the objective of peaceful agreement in the search for the common good, which is the true purpose of human life."

When the Communists announced that, at Whitsuntide

[10] See Document 10, "A Question of Changing Men."

1950, they planned a demonstration and a march in Berlin, Frank Buchman was invited to hold a mass meeting in the Ruhr at the same time, as a demonstration of an ideological answer. Dr. Adenauer welcomed the idea and wrote to Buchman: "I believe that in view of the offensive of totalitarian ideas in the East of Germany, the Federal Republic, and within it the Ruhr, is the given platform for a demonstration of the idea of Moral Re-Armament." [11]

So before three thousand miners, steelworkers, industrialists, and political leaders from all parts of Western Germany, Buchman made his speech. He chose as his theme "The Destiny of East and West." Beyond the walls of Gelsenkirchen's Hans Sachs Haus, the great hall which is a center of trade unionism in the Ruhr, millions listened as the speech went out over every West German radio station. The Western Berlin radio took it to the marchers in the streets and far beyond them to the East.

With Frank Buchman on the platform * were the former Communists, Bladeck, Kurowski, Benedens, Stoffmehl, and their friends, and at their side were Ruhr industrialists. They all spoke with one voice. After three hours the chairman tried to close the meeting. But hundreds of people would not leave. They stood round the platform clamoring for more.

The words of Frank Buchman at Gelsenkirchen struck a deep note in the hearts of those who heard him. "Unity," he said, "is our one hope. It is the destiny of France and Germany today. It is the destiny of East and West. The alternative is divide and die. Moral Re-Armament offers the world the last chance for every nation to change and survive, to unite and live."

---

[11] See Document 11, "I Welcome Your Plan," for full text of letters from Chancellor Adenauer and Minister-President Karl Arnold.

* Also on the platform were Mme. Aung San, widow of the late Premier, General Aung San of Burma; Mr. Etsuo Kato, President of the Japanese Railway Workers' Union: Senator Theodore F. Green of Rhode Island; and Mr. Hans Dütting, Managing Director of the Gelsenkirchen group of mines in the Gelsenkirchen Coal Company. Dr. Hermann Katzenberger, the Director of the Bundesrat at Bonn, was in the chair.

VI. CLASS WAR SUPERSEDED

•

The issue of world control will in the end be decided by the workers of the world. The struggle to capture the heart of the masses is the basic ideological battle.

Many people are misled by the parliament fortunes of the side they favor or hate. But Harry Pollitt, leader of the British Communist Party, saw the issues more clearly. In February 1950, after the electoral tide had wholly submerged his hundred parliamentary candidates, he stated: "The great issues will be settled, not in the arena of this reactionary Parliament, but by the workers' mass struggle in the factories and the streets."

In this battle there are key salients. The way that the dockers, coal miners, and shop stewards decide to move can settle the fate of a nation. And nowhere are these issues more vital today than in Britain, struggling for her economic survival.

I

The docks are the arteries of the world. Through them pumps the lifeblood of nations. In this ideological age the dockers of the world have mighty power. They can swiftly strangle the economy of a nation. Swiftly, too, they can girdle the globe with the answer that all men are looking for.

Dockers are, from the nature of their calling, a world brotherhood. So many pairs of hands, black, white, yellow, brown, handle the same cargoes of kegs and cases, sacks and casks that pass through the ports.

Not long ago a Liverpool docker dropped his wallet into the hold of a ship. It was too late and too difficult to recover it from among the cargo before the ship sailed. So the docker chalked on the hatch "Wallet lost in hold." Sure enough, it came back to him from the other side of the world. That is typical of the international family of dockers.

For more than eighty years the British docks have been a battleground. In 1889, under the leadership of Ben Tillett, the London dockers fought to establish the right of organization for unskilled workers. It was Ben who on his deathbed a few years ago sent the message to Frank Buchman: "You have a great international movement. Use it. It is the hope of to-morrow. Your movement will bring sanity back to the world."

The world dockers have the solidarity and the militancy of a family that for a long time has had to struggle, often to the point of bloodshed, for social justice, and have become accustomed to defending each other's interests under attack. The dockers have warm hearts and hot heads and they respond swiftly to any appeal to help the underdog.

The strength of the appeal of Communism to many of the dockers is that it is represented as a champion of social justice for the ordinary man and as a force against victimization.

The case is made more convincing by the fact that there are genuine grievances which need to be corrected. And the Communists fight hard to right these wrongs. But the warm hearts of the dockers—though the mass of them do not know it—are often exploited and used not for social justice, but for purposes of class warfare. The work of Moral Re-Armament in the docks aims to win men to an ideology based on absolute moral standards and the guidance of God.

Jack Manning of the Transport and General Workers' Union was a leading member of the London Port Workers' Committee until his resignation in October 1950. This committee, though unofficial, is a force in the docks. In the last two years they have brought about two major strikes supported by thousands of dockers in direct opposition to the policy of the national trade unions and the Labour Government.

Manning was also the manager of the *Port Workers' News*, which, he said, made the *Daily Worker* look as conservative as *The London Times*.

Manning's family have been connected with the docks for 120 years. His great-grandfather took part in the first unofficial strike on the London waterfront. Jack Manning says, "Before I met Moral Re-Armament there was only one person right—Jack Manning! When I was wrong, I said I was right."

Four times during the war the Manning home was smashed by bombs. "I had hatred," says Manning. "I believed the people who caused wars were the business class—money-grabbers we call 'em in Dockland."

A Manning son was killed fighting on the beaches in Normandy. Before he died he wrote home: "Dear Dad, I did not think I would see France this way. But if I give my life, carry on the fight where I left off so that the youth of the world may never have to fight a war again."

Jack Manning met Moral Re-Armament late in 1949 at a meeting in Canning Town Public Hall in the heart of the Dockland area. He came in the most quizzical frame of mind, ready to leave or to break up the proceedings if he disagreed with the speakers. He refused a seat and stood at the back of the hall leaning up against a radiator. But he was gripped from the start, and when he heard a representative of the "boss class," the Managing Director of a North of England tannery, telling the story of drastic change in his own life and business, Manning said to himself, "This is it." He stayed to talk two hours after the meeting.

He says, "I found in Moral Re-Armament what I had been looking for for a long time. A classless society that, if put into practice, could mean that war could never come again. I thought, 'Well, if I want some other fellow to change, start changing myself.' To change myself, that was a difficult job. For me, who was always right, to admit that I was sometimes wrong."

The Mannings began to live Moral Re-Armament in their home and at work. In the spring of 1950 an incident arose. Crates of matches were being loaded by crane. The foreman told the men to load more crates at each hoist than the men felt was safe. A quarrel broke out and one of the dockers hit the foreman.

The wharf manager discharged the docker and told him he would not be employed again on that wharf. The dockers contended this was contrary to the Dock Labour Scheme, under which disciplinary action can only be taken through the Dock Board. Immediately several hundred men went on strike and it seemed likely the dispute would spread.

At this point Jack Manning took a hand. It should be borne in mind that Manning played a leading part in the *Beaverbrae* strike in 1949 * and has been near the heart of many disturbances in Dockland.

As Jack and his wife, Nellie, talked it over, Jack had the thought to make a special visit to the wharf where the trouble was. "But it will mean losing a day's work," he said to Nellie. His wife answered, "If you are going to fight for an idea, you have got to sacrifice." So he went down to the wharf. Here is the story in his own words:

"I first went to the foreman who had been hit. He would not listen. He was sure he was right. Then I went to the man who had hit him and he wouldn't listen either. Then I went to the wharf manager. I told him: 'The man thinks you are wrong. You think the man is wrong. I think you are both wrong. But *I* may be wrong. The only way to settle this is to see what is right.' The manager thought for a few minutes and then said, 'Well, I must admit I was wrong.' " The manager thereupon reopened negotiations. He called a meet-

* This strike involved fifteen thousand men and tied up ninety-one ships in the Port of London for five weeks.

ing of trade union officials. The case was fully argued. On the basis of doing what was right instead of fighting over who was right, the ban on the employment of the man at that wharf was withdrawn. He was taken on again. Both sides agreed to allow the operation of the usual Dock Labour Board machinery, and all the men at once went back to work.

Tom Christie, of Glasgow, Chairman of the Dockers' Branch of the Scottish Transport and General Workers' Union, was one of the thirty-six dockers from Britain who attended the 1950 Caux Assembly. "Caux hit me like a rocket," he says. "I've tried it. It works. Thousands of people have been telling me for years that I needed to change. I said to them, 'You change first.' But at Caux everyone agreed to begin with themselves. This was a new idea. It's not an easy road but it's a good road. The old methods had succeeded in smashing my home. I blamed the wife for everything. But the change idea has worked. We are building things up again and have begun to refurnish the home with the money I used to spend in other ways. My sister says, 'If it works for you, Tom, it'll work anywhere.' "

Tom Christie and James McLaren, Secretary of the Dockers' Branch of the Scottish Transport and General Workers' Union, who also was at Caux, meet the employers' representatives every week to fix rates and settle grievances. McLaren says, "We used to go in looking for a fight. But on the basis of 'What's right' everyone gets the benefit." "Only yesterday," said Christie, taking up the story, "one of the employers actually *offered* to increase the rates for the job."

He added, "MRA is a priority for Britain. They can have all the parties and plans they want, but at the end of the day the statesmen of Britain will have to accept the four moral standards of MRA. The dockers have got plenty of fight. What we need is an idea worth fighting for. Now it is on the way. When the international force of dockers really gets behind this answer, nothing can stop it. This is the direct road to the new world."

Tom Christie also describes how he took a leading part in two of the greatest strikes in Britain during recent years. "They tied up the whole economic life of the island," he says. "It is a lot harder to accept the guidance of God than to pick the easy way of revolution. But by doing so you lead the working class to better conditions without creating poverty. I shall never again lead men out on strike without first of all applying the four standards of Moral Re-Armament."

Between November 1949 and July 1950 there were eight meetings for Moral Re-Armament in the London dock area, as well as rallies in Glasgow, Liverpool, and other parts of the country. These were largely attended by rank-and-file dockers and full-time dockers' union officials as well as by the unofficial leadership.

In the spring of 1951, Communist dockers, inspired by suggestions which came from Warsaw, attempted to pull out all the British docks on strike. They went to Merseyside and told the dockers there that, if they struck, London and Glasgow would support them. Merseyside struck.

Communist agents then went to London and Glasgow to attempt to bring the dockers there out in sympathy. For a whole week they struggled to do so. They had one hundred men marching up and down outside the dock gates as the men went to work early in the morning. They visited the homes of the dockers. They addressed them in mass meetings.

But the MRA-trained dockers' leaders, many of whom had led the big dock strikes of the last twenty years, publicly declared that this was not a strike for economic motives but an "ideological" effort to undermine the economy of Britain.

In Scotland not one docker struck. In London, out of twenty-seven thousand dockers only four hundred followed the Communist Party orders. One of the Communist leaders telephoned to Merseyside and informed his friends that it was Moral Re-Armament which had caused the efforts to bring about a strike to fail.

A government official said, "Moral Re-Armament are the

only people doing anything to deal with the problems of the dockers." And J. H. Sayne wrote in his column in the weekly paper, *East Europe*, "Moral Re-Armament have begun to out-wit the Communists . . . in the docks. They have won many of the key militant figures in the docks to their ideology."

Tom Keep is a typical example. He was a Communist for twenty-two years. He has been one of the principal strike leaders in the docks since the war. Keep himself was won to what he calls a "bigger idea" by the change in his manager.

Speaking publicly at the time of the attempted strike, Keep said, "For the first time I am speaking from the dictation of my conscience and not from a party line. . . . I learned and taught class hatred and revenge. Capitalism and Communism cannot be reconciled unless we find something to bridge the widening gap between them. . . . With the application of ab-solute moral standards comes the end of class war and with that comes the end of all war. Atrocities have come from the materialism both of the right and of the left. . . . If ever we needed a united world, it is now. Here is an ideology that fits into the life of people. It does not, like other ideologies, make people fit into them. This is the way to the emancipation of the workers. We can change the course away from fear and unemployment to peace and security."

When the danger of a stoppage had passed, ten of the dock-ers' leaders sent a copy of the English edition of this book to all 625 Members of the British House of Commons and the 827 Members of the House of Lords with a letter which read, "Our history is well known. Some of us are best known for our actions in past disputes in the docks. Up to 1950 some of us thought it impossible for the dockworkers to be wrong in any dispute that might arise in the industry. Then we met the force of Moral Re-Armament and they gave us something completely new. Among other things, as rank-and-file Trade Unionist officials, they taught us to fight even harder but on a new basis to that which we had previously adopted and that future actions should be determined on 'what is right' and not 'who is right.' We are proud to state we have adopted this line of fighting, so much so it is altering the thinking of the docks and us as well."

In the United States the journal, *Master, Mate and Pilot*, commented in an article in its February 1951 issue on this development in Dockland: "There are still just grievances to be put right. The question is—how can the dockers do this without exposing themselves to exploitation by militant materialism? And that question is being answered right now in the docks of Britain by an idea far superior to Communism, an idea of their own choosing which is winning the hearts and minds of the dockers. This is the idea, or ideology, of Moral Re-Armament, which punches holes in every form of materialism, either of right or left."

The aim of Moral Re-Armament is to build a leadership in the docks that fully understands the ideological nature of the battle for control; and to fight for moral change and the creation of new unity between trade unionists long hostile to each other. In many cases skilled Communists spend the early hours of the morning indoctrinating the dockers' leaders, while the Moral Re-Armament workers are there in the dockers' homes in the evening offering a still more revolutionary program. This battle has been going on for days, weeks, and months. Dockers know that the battle for social and economic change has not yet been fully won. But many of them begin to understand that if you fight for social and economic change alone, without also fighting for the moral change in every class, that is not revolutionary, but reactionary.

Marx said, "Capitalism contains the seeds of its own defeat." But many dockers now say that the workers' movements also contain the seeds of their own defeat unless they can find the cure for bitterness, jealousy, greed, and hate, and the answer to division among themselves.

The battle in the docks goes on daily.

After his visit to Caux, Bill Hegarty, then President of the

Stevedores' and Dockers' Union, was attacked by another
docker who hated Moral Re-Armament. Hegarty replied:
"Some of you fellows are like chameleons. When you are
with the Reds, you're red. When you are with the Blues,
you're blue. But I think you're just yellow."

Another dockers' leader says Moral Re-Armament has
meant three things to him:

(1) After three years' separation from his wife, his
    home is reunited.
(2) He, like other dockers in Caux, found his way back
    to the Catholic faith after years of absence.
(3) He is fighting daily for a sound ideology in the
    docks.

II

One of the main cargoes which fills the holds of the ships
in British ports is coal. If it is true that those who control the
docks can control the economic life of the world, it is also
true that those who control coal can control the economic
life of Britain. So the coalfields, like the docks, are a violent
ideological battlefield. The Foreign Minister of Britain, as far
back as 1947, remarked: "Give me coal and I will give you a
foreign policy."

Mr. Hugh Gaitskell, the Chancellor of the Exchequer, said
when he was Minister of Fuel and Power that the National
Coal Board had two tasks, a technical one and a psychological
one: "They had to achieve immense changes in the pits and
they had to change completely the spirit of those working
in the industry." It is in the second sphere that Moral Re-
Armament has made its impact on the coal industry.

When *The Forgotten Factor* was shown for nine months
in the Westminster Theatre in London, miners from the
different coalfields introduced the play each night from the
stage. As the audience broke up to meet the cast and talk, the
theater sounded with the soft burr of the Midlands, the lively

voice of Yorkshire, the singsong of Wales, and the slow rolling tones of Lancashire. Again and again miners from all over Britain traveled to London at their own expense to see the play—and often went back on the midnight trains so as to be ready for the morning shift.

Invitations were received from one hundred and fifty collieries in every part of the British coalfields to take the play there. And seventy thousand in the mining areas saw the play when it traveled to Yorkshire and the Midlands, to Scotland and to North and South Wales.

Harold Lockett, Secretary of the North Staffordshire miners and a member of the National Executive of the National Union of Mineworkers, summed up the effects as follows: "When Moral Re-Armament comes in, Communism goes out, production goes up, absenteeism goes down. This spirit in every coalfield would ensure national recovery."

A typical case of the effects of the application of MRA was at the Victoria Pit, North Staffordshire. *The Stoke Sentinel* of October 29, 1947, reported that the pit had set up an all-time record for the pit in coal-raising of 11,075 tons a week. The original target was 8,000 tons. This was raised first to 9,000 then to 10,000 tons. Referring to this increase in production, Bill Yates, National Union of Mineworkers' President for the pit, said, "Since seeing *The Forgotten Factor* with my workmates my eyes were opened as to where I could play my part. Since then co-operation between men and management has never been greater." During the last three years Bill Yates has:

(1) Created a new spirit in his pit.
(2) Worked with officials in the Area Coal Board in the fight for a united industry.
(3) Helped to create a panel of miners' spokesmen who have carried to the statesmen and industrial leaders of nine countries the ideology they have worked out in their pits.

The twenty-one NUM Branch Secretaries in North Staffordshire sent an illuminated address to Frank Buchman thanking him for the new teamwork Moral Re-Armament had brought into their area. One of them, Aaron Colclough, of Glebe Colliery, says, "Before MRA came to our pit, we had never once hit our production target. In the weeks following the showing of *The Forgotten Factor* we beat the target so regularly that the Coal Board in co-operation with the miners raised it."

Commenting on this development, the *Birmingham Post* said, "The new spirit is so revealing itself in increased output that, according to one computation based on recent figures, if the same results were obtained in all British coalfields, the target of 200 millions tons a years (1947) would be exceeded by 30 million tons."

In many cases a decisive change in the attitude of the manager was the key to new co-operation for the men. In one of the largest and most modern pits in Britain the manager, Spencer Hughes, used to be known as the "Pocket Battleship" by the men, on account of his size and nature. Shortly after he had been influenced by Moral Re-Armament it was noticed that the weekly output of his pit had risen from 13,000 to 17,000 tons a week. Asked what had caused the rise he said, "That play, *The Forgotten Factor*, taught me to apologize and look on the whole of my work quite differently." A year later he wrote that the upward trend was maintained and that the 20,000-ton mark was being exceeded —all this without extra manpower or new machinery. The output is now around the 21,000-ton level.

Of the effect of *The Forgotten Factor* on the South Wales coalfield, Jack Jones, the author of *Rhondda Roundabout*, says, "This forgotten factor which demands a change of heart from everyone has pierced the armour plate of every ideology from Conservative to Communist and set thousands on the new road."

Mr. Tom Beacham, the Area Production Officer for the

pits in the Rhondda (No. 3 Area, Western Division, National Coal Board), dates a marked improvement from about the time that *The Forgotten Factor* was shown there. He wrote, "It has had a great effect on our relationships which is showing itself in the negotiations between the Board and the Union. The big problem everywhere is to get co-operation at pit level, and this is doing it. There is not the acrimony and bitterness there was. The Welsh collier is a realist and likes to see things work out practically. Men are quick to sense any change in management."

William M. Arthur, General Secretary, NUM, South Wales, and William Hopkins, Chairman, TUC South Wales Advisory Committee, and National President of the General and Municipal Workers' Union, summed up the visit of *The Forgotten Factor* by saying, "It has been successful beyond our dreams. Its spirit will have a great and abiding effect on our valleys."

Peter O'Connor from Scotland who, before he was killed at his pit, twice crossed the Atlantic to tell American industrial and Congressional leaders of the results of MRA in the British mines, declared: "Miners digging more coal alone will not save Britain. Miners guided by God and working together with the fire of an ideology will save democracy."

Tom Gunn, a Branch Secretary in the National Union of Mineworkers in Scotland, was faced with the closing down of his pit by the Coal Board due to low output. The miners were only digging half a ton per man-shift. After seeing *The Forgotten Factor* he realized that he had been leading his men wrongly. He decided to change his attitude and ask the Coal Board for a few months to work out absolute moral standards on the job. The manager and he operated together on this new basis and have done so ever since. Production rose from half a ton to 1.2 tons per man. The pit has remained open, and the miners have lost their fear of having families split up and homes broken. The manager and Tom Gunn no longer regard each other as enemies.

John Colthart, Assistant Labour Director for the NCB, Scottish Division, who was formerly Vice-President of the Scottish miners, says that he uses the achievements of these two men (O'Connor and Gunn) as an example for every pit in Scotland.

Over one hundred miners' leaders from Great Britain have been as spokesmen and for training to the World Assembly at Caux. They have visited Norway, Sweden, Denmark, Holland, and the United States, the French coalfields and the Ruhr, and have told industrialists, Cabinet Ministers, and labor leaders in those countries what is happening in Britain. The miners themselves have started a fighting fund to which all can contribute to send their spokesmen wherever the needs of the world and their own conviction should lead them.

To celebrate the tenth anniversary of Moral Re-Armament, the President and Secretary of the NUM, North Staffordshire, the Agent and Secretary of the NUM, Leicestershire, and the President of the NUM, Warwickshire, invited leaders of the mining industry from France, Germany, Belgium, and Holland to a national demonstration to celebrate the occasion.[12]

Frank Painter, President of the Warwickshire miners says, "We had no ideology at all in the British coal industry except that of materialism. But Moral Re-Armament has brought a better idea. It has not only given real teamwork and better output, but it has sent many miners like myself across the world to give evidence of an answer, tried and tested in our British coalfields, and now given to the nations."

III

Apart from the dockers and miners, the shop stewards on the floor of the factories are key figures in the ideological battle to control industry.

[12] See Document 12, "Ideology in the Pits."

Shop stewards are rank-and-file workers, elected by their fellows to represent them. They do the day-to-day negotiations in the factory and have the opportunity to settle or to magnify many disputes at their outset. Many of them have a passion for social justice and a desire to conquer the apathy of the masses of the workers and restore enthusiasm for trade unionism.

Following the visit of the MRA plays to London and the centers of heavy industry, shop stewards and trade union leaders in these areas started to plan ideological training courses. One of these was a course recently given in Birmingham and attended by over a hundred shop stewards belonging to fourteen unions and twenty-two factories employing over one hundred thousand workers, including Austin, Morris Commercial, Birmingham Small Arms, Lucas, General Electric Company, Cadbury, and Guest, Keen and Nettlefold. It is interesting to note that, at the time of writing, no major strike has taken place for two years in the departments or factories for which these men are responsible. Similar courses have taken place in Belfast, South Wales, Yorkshire, Merseyside, Clydeside, and the London area.

Albert Burr, in June 1951, reported on the situation in the Dunlop Rubber Company's factory at Fort Dunlop, where he is Chairman of Shop Stewards. Since the war, he said, labor relations had been a "cat and dog" affair. Then in 1950 the works superintendent, the Shop Stewards Convener, Burr, and a leading Communist went to Caux. Up to that time the company had not recognized the shop stewards committee. But after Caux, when they saw the way the men were applying their new experience, the company decided to meet the stewards. Within a few hours the men's grievances, which had been piling up for eighteen months, were settled. The men received an immediate increase of over $80,000 a year. In return the men admitted that they had for thirty years been applying restrictive practices to prevent production ever passing a certain limit. They promised to abandon these practices.

Management guaranteed that, as production increased, wages would keep pace.

John Reynolds is a Member of the National Executive Committee of the Transport and General Workers' Union. He is a convener of shop stewards in Birmingham, was for many years an active member of the Communist Party, and when he was in Moscow stood on the same platform as Stalin. Of this training for shop stewards Reynolds said in August 1950, "The wonderful thing about Moral Re-Armament is that we do not wait for a Utopia but set about the job here and now. In my home we are holding training classes. My home is just two attic rooms in one of the main thoroughfares of the city of Birmingham. It is scanty of furniture but there is a certain amount of hospitality for any of my friends who care to come. To that simple home have come some of the top management of Birmingham. They have sat on my sofa. We have discussed the problems of industry and we have found solutions to these problems."

Arthur Morrell works in the British plant of the Ford Motor Company at Dagenham, and until the spring of 1951 was shop steward convener responsible for sixteen thousand men. He says, "My own superintendent and I were for a long time very bitter enemies over a wrong I was convinced he had done me. For many years I did my utmost against him by causing all the trouble I could. Then I met Moral Re-Armament. The first thing I had to do was the most difficult I could think of: to go and apologize to the superintendent. To be perfectly frank, I do not think I had ever apologized to anybody in my life before then. After walking back and forth fifteen times, I finally plucked up enough courage to go into his office and apologize. Someone told me a few days later that he remarked, 'If Moral Re-Armament can do that to Morrell, there is something there. I am going to have a look at it.' Moral Re-Armament can change people. It can change a worker. It can change management. MRA has meant a lot of difference to Ford's. It has been said by the Chairman of

Ford's himself that this year (1949–50) has been the best year for negotiations in his experience. It has been a record year in car production. That is a by-product of MRA, in my opinion. Moral Re-Armament is giving the spirit that brings co-operation between the management and men, and then extra production comes automatically. Then increase in pay arises from the increase in production."

Morrell's superintendent is Bill Whatham, who has had thirty-six years' service with the company and is in charge of fifteen hundred men in the assembly building. He was British Wrestling Champion in 1923, and used to feel that no holds are barred in the battle for production. He says: "In the un-settled conditions after the war I tried the tough way with the men. We had stoppages, strikes, and go-slows. It did not work. Then the shop stewards in the assembly building asked me if I would meet them to discuss our problems on the basis of the moral standards of MRA. I agreed. There is no agenda. No minutes are kept. No punches are pulled. And I am glad to say that so far every issue brought forward has been set-tled on a basis of right."

Results have been remarkable. On the eight- and ten-horse-power assembly line, for example, production was 107 cars behind one week early in 1951 due to shortage of material. Whatham, Morrell, and their men went to work with such co-operation that the loss was made up in record time. The efficiency of this assembly line, on a time study basis, was 97% in February 1951—the highest since the war. In April it was 99.43%. In May it had risen to 100.4%.

"Some months ago I was given responsibility for the Export Shipping Department," Whatham adds. "At that time the men in this section were working an hour and a half over-time every night, as well as every Saturday and three Sundays in each month. The first thing that happened was that my old shop stewards in the assembly building had a talk with the shop stewards from this new section and told them how we work together. The result is that today we work no overtime."

Instead of being two and a half days behind on the job, we are now two and a half days ahead, and the men have received pay benefits."

The *Communist Review* published a complaint that the hold which Moral Re-Armament had on sections in the Dagenham works was adding to their difficulties in infiltrating Ford's.

When Mrs. Henry Ford [13] died at the end of September 1950, the following message was sent from the Ford plant at Dagenham:

"We Ford employees wish to send a message of sympathy to the family of Mrs. Henry Ford. We recognise in her a fellow fighter and pioneer for Moral Re-Armament. MRA has united us in heart and spirit though we work in different grades. It has introduced a new factor into Management-Labor negotiations. It has made the class war as old-fashioned and unnecessary as an outmoded industrial process. It is the way for the second half of the Twentieth Century."

James Leask is a Birmingham trades union leader, responsible for sixty thousand men in the engineering industry. But at one time he was cynical about them and about the future. Leask saw in Moral Re-Armament the world that in his heart he and all his comrades wanted.

In a broadcast debate on the BBC with Willie Gallacher, Chairman of the British Communist Party, Leask said, "The ideology of Communism is inadequate for the needs of the twentieth century. In ideological warfare the Communists can show us much. They have a passion, a plan, and a philosophy which many of us need. The trade union's job is to unite. The real forces of reaction are those who refuse to change. The new world will not come through liquidation but through change. The choice is between materialistic dictatorship and free people. In the world today there is a battle for the minds of men. The ideas that are biggest will

[13] See Document 13, "Hope for the Future," statement by Mr. Henry Ford in 1939.

win. The need is for a coalition of all the sound forces to build for all time a better world for everyone."

Men from forty-nine British Trades Unions and twenty-five Trades Councils have been to Caux.[14] New voices are being heard in works councils, district and national union committees. Resolutions reflect a new vision for industry to feed, clothe, and house the millions, and a new passion for unity and the fulfillment of the destiny of the workers of the world.

Frank Buchman has said that labor led by God can lead the world. That is the revolutionary conception of Moral Re-Armament. Many West German Marxists say, "This is what Socialists have been looking for for a hundred years." The President of the Berlin Trade Unions, Scharnowski, said, "Tell Frank Buchman that I will be fighting with him in Berlin. These are the ideas we need, for class warfare today is out of date." The chief Workers' Delegate for Britain at the ILO said, as he left Caux, "Absolute moral standards must become the driving force of the workers of the world."

In the last century the cry was "Workers of the world, unite." The urgent need was to unite against something, against injustice and poverty, which existed then and still exist. But the need today is "Workers unite the world," with a great positive idea. That is why the leaders of world labor come to Caux.[15] That is why one hundred labor leaders from the inaugural conference of the International Confederation of Free Trade Unions in 1949, including their President, Paul Finet, came to the headquarters of MRA in London. And that is why the veteran European trade union leader, Evert Kupers, says, "I march with Frank Buchman, shoulder to shoulder, to that better society in which shall reign social security and social justice." [16]

[14] See Document 14, "The Dilemma of Labor."
[15] See Document 15, "World Industrial Conference.'
[16] See Document 16, "World Labor and Caux."
See also Document 29, "Labor's Destiny."

VII. NEW FACTOR IN MANAGEMENT

•

Just as in the docks and mines and factories workers are changing and fighting for Moral Re-Armament, so among employers on a world front can be seen the forging of an ideological force.

In a lecture to Communist leaders in Moscow Stalin once said, "If capitalism could adapt its production not to getting maximum profits but to the systematic improvement of the masses of the people, then there would not be any crisis—but then capitalism would not be capitalism."

Stalin clearly regards the changing of capitalists as unlikely. But something of which he never dreamed is now beginning to enter into human affairs. It is the fact that the motives and hearts of men can be changed. Frank Buchman gives the keynote for a new age with his words, "Human nature can be changed. That is the basic answer. National economies can be changed. That is the fruit of the answer. World history can be changed. That is the destiny of our age."

MRA does not aim to change capitalists in order to prop up an existing economic system. It aims to change all men to the place where they are willing to pledge their lives, their fortunes, and their sacred honor in the fight for a rebuilt world.

When capitalists change and when, as often follows, Marxists and workers change also, a new and fruitful harmony is created in which everyone has a part and from which all benefit. It is a dynamic unity produced when capitalist and worker begin to see a new range and purpose for the whole of their efforts—not profits and wages, not a battle for control, but a united determination that the work and wealth of the world become available for all and for the exploitation of none.

I

Here are the words of Mr. John Nowell, General Manager of the Camden Tannery, Runcorn, England, and President of the National Association of Cut Sole Manufacturers.

"Unless we in management accept the challenge of Marxist thinking, we shall miss the challenge of our age and we shall be completely outdated. . . . Management must change. Many of us feel we have done our duty if we make it easy for workers to change. We approve. We support. We patronize. But we are slow to change. For myself, I can be a man of ideals. I can show great benevolence and even share my profits. But if I don't change, it counts for little. The structure of materialism rests very largely on the fact that there is a reactionary Right. The reactionary is one who will not change. Change begins to build a new structure. . . . The challenge is to remake the world."

Camden Tannery has built up its reputation over a quarter of a century. It processes two hundred thousand hides a year and produces from them seven million pounds of good shoe leather.

Some years ago a strike was organized in the works by a shop steward named Tom Tattersall. He was regarded as a difficult man. The foreman used to remark, "I keep a pretty good eye on Tattersall. In fact, I keep both eyes."

When the stoppage occurred, John Nowell realized that someone had to take initiative in breaking down the suspicion that existed everywhere in the place. He sent for Tattersall. He said he was sorry that he had distrusted workers in general and Tom in particular. This had, he felt, made it impossible for Tom to co-operate.

Nowell said he wanted to put all his cards on the table from now on and fight together with Tom for what was right. The shop steward was dubious but decided to give it a try. "In a new atmosphere free from tension," says Nowell, "we were able to sit down and work out what changes were needed on both sides."

A works council was set up which for the last years has been the mainstay of all the discipline in the factory and acted as a forum where ideas could be discussed. Since then not one pound of production has been lost through friction. Avoidable absenteeism has been at the rate of one hour in a thousand. And although there has been constantly changing raw material, which has meant the movement of men into different jobs with fluctuating wage rates, there has been no dispute, and the work has gone smoothly on.

The trade union's district organizer said, "There is here a clear example for the rest of industry. Every one of my four thousand members has benefited from what I have learned at the Tannery."

When during a period of acute labor shortage their manpower was reduced by twenty-five per cent, the remainder worked so well that production did not suffer. "In this amazingly increased productivity of men who are happy and free, I see the only hope of the democracies adequately increasing their defenses without becoming bankrupt in the process and so risking revolution from within by the loss of their standard of living," said Nowell.

Nowell described the case of a young man who came to the Tannery from a good Christian home. He had applied for a clerical job but through a misunderstanding was put on to manual labor. This was the first of a number of unfortunate incidents culminating in the refusal of the firm, for what were in their opinion very proper reasons, to let him take his wife for a holiday which had been ordered by the doctor. The young man became bitter and turned to Communism. "It was this story, when I came to hear of it, that brought home very forcibly to me the responsibility of management," says Nowell. "It was not viciousness on our part but just blindness. We are so often blind and insensitive because we put plans, production, and profits—all legitimate things, all necessary things—before people." Nowell adds, "It was the change in me which won the young man back to a sound democratic ideology."

It is interesting that Nowell's change of attitude toward industry began at home. He says he and his wife seemed sometimes only "to span a great chasm of misunderstanding by the frail bridge of politeness." Then one day he decided to tell his wife what he was really like. It was the beginning of a new teamwork between the two. A little later his wife said to him, "Why don't you be honest with the men at the Tannery as you are with me?"

Nowell describes the spirit of the plant as "revolutionary teamwork." "It is not the teamwork of those who agree," he explains, "but the teamwork of those who disagree, the teamwork of those who clash and change. It is the new dialectics. The chief shop steward in our works said one day to a visitor from abroad, 'We still have our problems, but where they used to lead to conflict and deadlock they now lead to change and progress.'"

And it was the revolutionary change in Nowell, as the head of a firm and an employer of labor, which first captured the imagination of some of the leaders of the London dockers and enlisted them in MRA when Nowell was a speaker at one of the mass meetings for dockers in the East End of London.

Another British industrialist is Mr. Eric Robey, the president of a national association dealing with building materials. When the government appealed to industry to keep prices down, Robey's conviction was for his own industry to consider what price reductions they could make in the national interest.

He met with opposition, but the force of his own conviction and the way in which he fought the matter as a moral issue carried the day. Lower prices were approved and put into use, thus lowering the cost of building repairs throughout the country.

Shortly afterwards a government report was published criticizing the industry for their methods and recommending increased government control. The minister in charge said in the House of Commons that before the report had been presented, the industry itself had voluntarily reduced a number of its prices. No further action was taken.

Mr. Ernesto G. Diederichsen, a textile manufacturer from Brazil, says this,[17] "Management has to change. We have to change to live out the ideology of Moral Re-Armament. This ideology has three characteristics. First, it is world-wide in scope. Secondly, it makes clear that 'As I am, so is my nation, and so is my factory.' Thirdly, it shows that there is a plan for each of us: a plan for management, a plan for labor."

II

When management is gripped with an ideology of change, the workers swiftly respond. Take the case of the banker and the Communist. Hermann Hintzen, a director of one of the oldest banking houses in Europe, felt himself, in his own words, to be an "enlightened dictator, like Frederick the Great, at home and in the office." He began to change. One day he met Carlos Pronk, the fighting "progressive" leader who started the independent Marxist organization in Holland. The banker talked with Pronk for three hours and told him where he and other employers like himself had failed in their responsibility and how he now was resolved to fight for a new world.

Following a visit to Caux in 1950, Pronk, with the approval of his comrades, renamed his newspaper *The New World* and wrote in it, "Bitterness and hatred are understandable, but they are no basis for a new world. The people of the world can be more quickly united on the basis of MRA. A little

[17] See Document 17, "The New Priority for Industry."

more socialism applied in the family would be a better example than a thousand speeches to convince the neighbors."

He felt that he must be different at home, and become thereby "a better father for his children."

He said at Caux, "If atomic war comes, there will be neither capitalism nor socialism, but only barbarism. If we fight in the old way, we shall have ruin. But if we fight in the new moral way, a new world can come as different as light from darkness. A better world can only come through better men."

Another Dutch employer, Charles Redelé, is a producer of foodstuffs. He came to Caux in 1950. He says, "I had not many enemies but those I had were real ones. For nine years I had a feeling of real hate against one of my competitors. He has a smaller factory than mine but he was president of our organization in Holland. For nine years I tried to make it impossible for him to go on being president of our group."

Redelé decided to change. He went to see this hated competitor. The competitor did not want to see him and over the telephone told him he could not make an appointment for at least three weeks. "All right. Let's meet after three weeks," said Redelé. When they met, Redelé says, "I told him I was sorry for what I had done to him during nine years. I told him my reason was jealousy because I thought, as I owned one of the biggest factories of our kind of foodstuffs in Holland, I ought to be president. I asked his forgiveness for the dirty tricks I had played on him. And he was blowing his nose and trying not to let me see the tears in his eyes. He couldn't speak at all for two or three minutes. So we stood together shaking hands like two fools."

As a result of this interview, the president wrote to his former enemy, "This will undoubtedly have material as well as spiritual consequences. We must present it in the best way possible to our federation."

And the material consequences have already begun. After Charles Redelé changed, he told his workers he wanted them to take equal responsibility with him in serving the people.

Workers came to see him. They told him they knew it was possible to raise the output of the factory twenty per cent. If the workers did that, what, they asked, would Redelé do? Would the extra twenty per cent in production go to increasing the profits of the concern, and to the shareholders? Or would he be willing to use it to decrease the price of the food to the public and so lower the cost of living in Holland? Redelé agreed to the second course and the workers agreed to attempt an extra twenty per cent in production.

In the following eight months Redele's firm have on three occasions been able to lower the prices of some of their products, in spite of the increasing costs of raw materials. "What is even more interesting," says Redele, "is that everyone finds much more joy in his work. Instead of just feeling they are putting biscuits from a pan into tins all day long, the workers know that they are helping to solve one of the biggest problems of Holland."

Recently some of the workers came to Redele and said, "Mr. Charles, what about your colleagues, manufacturers of shoes and clothing—why shouldn't they do for Holland what we are doing? Why don't we get them to visit the factory here? If you'll do the inviting, we'll do the talking when they come." Already a number have visited the factory to hear what Redele's workers have to say about bringing down the cost of living. A member of the Dutch Cabinet said to Redele, "What you tell me is the answer to our problems."

III

Bernard Hallward was President of the St. Raymond Paper Company, Canada. When he measured his life against absolute moral standards, he had to sit down and write a check for a large sum which he owed the Canadian customs. This made headline news in the Canadian press.

Hallward then began to see how moral compromise in men like himself had created the injustices of the Western world.

"I see," he says, "the hardness of the materialism of the right mirrored in the bitterness of the materialism of the left. Communism is the outcome of the neglected conscience of the West. If you see your face reflected in a mirror and don't like the look of it, it is no use throwing stones at the mirror. If you change your own appearance, there is a good chance that the reflection in the mirror will also change."

Hallward has traveled across the Atlantic fifteen times to help bring Moral Re-Armament to the European countries. In the Ruhr he is welcomed and beloved by many Marxist and Communist leaders. In 1949 he was one of the spokesmen at a meeting of one hundred and fifty Ruhr industrialists which went on for seven hours. Its aim was to plan how the spirit of Moral Re-Armament could be brought right through the Ruhr. Someone who knows German industry well said that if a bomb had fallen on that hall, Ruhr industry would have ceased because all the big employers of labor were present. They heard industrial and trade union voices from a dozen countries.

Dr. Heinrich Kost, Managing Director of the Rheinpreussen Company and Chairman of the German Coal Board, who had called the meeting, said: "It is necessary that division be put aside, and that instead of division unity come in. This will happen when we have the real desire and intention to change ourselves. We must put people first in our plan. In this way we can unite as human beings so that something happens not only in our business but in our community and in our Fatherland. It is not for us employers to wait for labor to change. Change, gentlemen, is demanded of us. It is not a question of whether we change but how we change."

Following this speech, Bladeck and Kurowski, the veteran Communists in his pits, went to see him. They raised grievances which had been outstanding for several years. In the spirit of Caux, all grievances were settled within half an hour.

Hans Dütting, managing director of another group of Ruhr coal mines, has twenty-five thousand men directly under him.

He says of Caux, "I have had to alter my whole idea of the nature and purpose of industry. Of course, we have to see that things are produced and distributed in the right way. We have to see that mankind has enough of the things they need. We also have to see that our workers have security and a better standard of living. But we have, above all, to be sure the workers and employers of the world have the certainty of inner satisfaction in their life. We have to remake the world. That is an idea for which it is worth not only working but sacrificing."

When Dütting first went back from Caux he talked to his men about Moral Re-Armament. To his surprise, nothing happened. They were not convinced. Then he saw that Moral Re-Armament, to be convincing, had to be lived, not just talked about. He began to change himself. This is the verdict of Paul Dikus, chairman of the works council for Dütting's group of mines: "Two years ago there was great tension. When Director Dütting first went to Caux we workers just laughed about it. I can only say that his change has completely bowled us over. A few years ago I did everything possible to try and prevent Director Dütting from being appointed to his present position. Now here I stand at Caux with him. I have been a Socialist for twenty-five years. The class war has been written on our banners. But I realize that is not the way to find a solution to the problems between management and labor. In our pit we are really demonstrating how you can bring the answer to all problems on the basis of what is fair for all, without resorting to class warfare. . . . Therefore I, as a worker, say an absolutely clear 'Yes' to Caux."

"Workers' control" is the battle cry of the Left in the Ruhr. Some of the employers are countering it with various forms of co-partnership. Others take a stand on their traditional rights as capitalists. What have Dikus and Dütting to say about this?

Dikus states, "Great discussions are going on in the Ruhr about the participation of workers in the running of business.

But with the relationship I have with our director that does not cause me any worries at all. I know that we have already got further through the relationship that we have reached together freely than other firms will get by means of a law."

Dütting says, "If we are really honest and unselfish, the workers' participation in control can be no problem to us. An employer who puts into practice absolute moral standards will give his workers more than any law can demand of him. And he can do so without hesitation because he knows that the employees' representatives also base their work on these same standards.

"We must give all everywhere an ideology built on absolute moral standards which is worth work and sacrifice," Dütting adds. "We can, workers and employers, stand firm against materialism wherever it comes from, West or East. We will have a new future."

IV

In France Robert Tilge is one of the many industrialists fighting for Moral Re-Armament. He is Secretary of the Employers' Federation of Northern France, which includes fourteen thousand industrial and fifty thousand commercial concerns and represents forty per cent of French heavy industry.

He is a massive man; played rugby football for his country and has wrestled in many international contests. His friends named him the Elephant, but the workers of France called him the Bulldog because he never lets go.

He is a human force. For years he battled for the rights of the employers. He became an inevitable part of any major industrial crisis in France. In one period of twelve months he had to deal with one hundred and sixty strikes.

But bitterness increased. Deadlock deepened. And Tilge, who is a patriot, saw his country spent and weakened in a struggle of which he was a part but for which he had no answer.

At Caux, Tilge changed. He went back home and addressed

an assembly of leaders of management and labor from all over the north of France. He apologized to the workers present for his wrong attitude toward them. That marked the beginning of an ideological offensive in French industry.

Meanwhile Robert Tilge himself has visited the USA, Canada, and many European countries with task forces of Moral Re-Armament.

Addressing four hundred leading business men in London in February 1950, he said, "You will say that no one of us is responsible for Communism. That is right, but aren't we and our fathers responsible for the climate of our country, for the social climate, and the resulting wave of Communism before which every nation trembles with fear?

"I sometimes think that Management is always late by one franc, one hour, one idea, because we have always been the people who want to keep and not to give. We must face our responsibility, in the factory, in the profession, in the nation, our responsibility for a falling civilization. Caux has shown me that we must start a fight with ourselves, a war with our own selfishness; then we shall be starting to stop the next war and to save culture and democracy."

v

In America the president of the company which made forty per cent of the dehydrated apples for the whole United States Army during the war, picked up a telephone one day and called the Packing House Workers' Union. "My name is Edgar Gallwey," he told the official. "Our workers want you to organize our factory. Please come and see me."

The secretary and business agent of the union called on the president of the factory. They were suspicious. Never in their experience had an American employer made such a move. Gallwey simply told them he wanted their help in establishing right relations between management and labor.

The union produced a seventeen-page contract. Gallwey

said that, while it was a good contract, it was built on the suspicion of both parties and designed to cover every loophole. At the suggestion of the union secretary he produced a one-and-a-half-page alternative contract, which was accepted. This was a simple statement on wage rates, union membership requirements, and vacations. It carried an undertaking to deal with any issues that might arise in a spirit of honesty and fairness.

A year later the president of the union told Gallwey, "I am prouder of this agreement than of any other contract our union has." The official newspaper of the American Federation of Labor described it as the most satisfactory working agreement in the state of California.

In the eight years since that time the company and the union have spent only a few hours in contract negotiation. There has been no stoppage or slowdown. The union has not been called on to take up a single major grievance with management.

The motive for both management and labor in that factory is the service of the people. There have been substantial wage increases. At the same time the company was able, in the middle of their contract, to cut their price to the government by fifteen per cent. Inventiveness among the workers was the greatest source of saving. One man, for example, had an idea which resulted in an increase of two million pounds of dehydrated fruit each year at an added cost of only three thousand dollars.

The board of directors at first felt it hard to back Gallwey's "all cards on the table" policy with the union. One particularly cautious director remained unconvinced until he called on Gallwey one day when a rush shipment of apples for the armed forces was being sent out. As the president and the director walked past the shipping line, Gallwey pointed to a man in his shirtsleeves hauling the heavy crates. "He is the business agent of the union you are so suspicious about," he told the director. The union official, who was not employed by the company, had come to collect union dues, seen the emergency, taken off his coat, and gone to work.

In the spring of 1948 the company received a serious setback. A large order was suddenly canceled, after the company had entered into financial commitments to meet it.

It was at the time when a new union contract was due to be signed and the union had been obtaining ten to fifteen per cent wage increases throughout the industry. The company was willing to increase wages, but the financial crisis required retrenchment.

As soon as the union representative knew the facts, he told Gallwey, "Maybe there is some way we can help." He suggested the contract should be signed with no wage increase but on the same basis as the previous year. Gallwey said this would help tremendously and insisted on putting a clause into the contract that he would keep the union advised of the company's position and that, if conditions improved before the end of the contract, he would reopen the question of wages.

A meeting was held by the employees and it was unanimously decided *not* to ask for any increase. Seven months after this, and five months before the contract expired, the company's position had so much improved, largely due to the interest of the employees and the effort they had made in preventing waste and helping cut costs, that the company was able to give a substantial wage increase to all employees.

At an industrial conference in October 1950, at Los Angeles, attended by business, labor, and industrial representatives from the USA, Canada, Europe and the Far East, Gallwey said, "This is an ideology—an idea put into practice. In American industry today we have to fight to produce not only the goods but the life that weaves the future of this country and the future of the world."

VI

The stories of change in employers of labor told in this section of the book are part of a rising tide of new thinking and living in many lands.

Today Moscow counts on the chronic selfishness of capitalists to bring about the downfall of Western civilization and to open the gateway for the triumph of Marxism.

Communists believe that the triumph of their cause is a hastening process of history. But history itself may record that the factor forgotten by Marx, hinted at by Stalin, in the end proved the decisive factor. That is the possibility of a change in the motive of employers themselves, the forging of an ideological force based on change and including changed management.

If this process were to take place, the core of the Marxist case would be broken.

And the fact is that such a process has now begun.

VIII. TOTAL PREPAREDNESS

•

Total war is one more manifestation of the ideological age. Today war involves peoples as well as armies, faiths as well as weapons, ideology as well as military strategy.

Moral Re-Armament recognized from 1939 onward, and put on record, that the democracies were, in fact, fighting two wars, "a war of arms and a war of ideas. Both are fought on a world front. And the eventual victor must win both wars." * Every year since the end of the war has underlined this truth. It has been evident in the relations between the occupying powers and the peoples of Germany and Japan; and still more in the advances made by Soviet Russia. Six European countries, Poland, Hungary, Rumania, Bulgaria, Albania, and Czechoslovakia, have been taken over. Neither armies nor atom bombs played the decisive part in these campaigns.

In China, as the Red Army moved southward, the undermining of the civilian population together with the much inferior morale of the Nationalist army, led to what was virtually a bloodless conquest of the greater part of the country. One of the Nationalist leaders said, "We lost the war on the ricefields, not the battlefields." The minds and wills of the Chinese people were won by a powerful ideology that penetrated far beyond the aircraft and the guns.

In Korea, Indo-China, Malaya, Burma, and Indonesia the force of this new factor is behind nearly every clash of the

* See *The Fight to Serve*, an account of the war service of MRA workers, page 9.

last five years. If successive defeats are to be avoided, it follows that this weapon must be confronted with the armament of a superior ideology.

The nation that neglects its ideological arm will lose even the peace it has won with its military arms. As Frank Buchman has said: "We have learned that democracy without an ideology can win a war but cannot build a peace; that ideological preparedness is the task of the whole nation, and is the one sure basis of national strength, moral, military and economic."

It was this that Lieutenant-General Touzet du Vigier had in mind in a speech he made at Caux in August 1950. He was former Chief of Staff to General de Lattre de Tassigny and wartime Commander of the French First Armored Division. He said, "Our security lies in the ideological vigor of the West. Every nation has three sorts of frontiers to defend: the political frontier which is determined by history, the strategic frontier marked out by geography, and now, more than ever, the ideological frontier which goes through the heart of every man."

I

Lieutenant-General du Vigier and Major-General de Vernejoul, of France, together with other senior officers from many countries who are interested in these new aspects of national and international defense, suggested that representatives of armed forces of the free nations should be invited to attend the Caux Assembly in September 1950. The Defense Ministers of four of the Atlantic Pact powers were officially represented, the Minister of Overseas Territories of France, and the High Commissioner for Pakistan in London. One hundred and two officers from sixteen countries attended. They included twenty-one officers of General rank and forty-seven of field rank, or its equivalent.

As they gathered, the foreign ministers of the Atlantic

Powers were meeting simultaneously in New York, with the problem of how to create an integrated European defense system high on their agenda.

Against this background a most significant feature of the Caux conference was the spirit of reconciliation that was generated between former enemies. In a matter of days a mental fusion occurred that overcame deep-rooted suspicions and paved the way for effective teamwork in technical planning. Former German officers were moved to apologize for their responsibility for the war. One German colonel offered to restore to France private property he had removed during the campaign there. The senior German officer present was the former General Hossbach. As chief adjutant of the Wehrmacht before the war Hossbach many times expressed openly his opposition to National Socialism.

During the war Hitler ordered Hossbach to allow his men to be circled by the Russians. Hossbach refused. Having extricated his men from the trap he flew home instead of to Berlin as ordered, barricaded himself indoors, and held out against the Gestapo until the Americans arrived.

One day General Hossbach heard a British officer, Rear-Admiral O. W. Phillips, speak. Admiral Phillips said he felt that his country must accept its share of responsibility for the way the world had gone. He said he was sorry that Britain had in the years between the wars lacked an idea powerful enough to bring change to herself and then to other nations. General Hossbach was moved by these unexpected words from a British admiral. He saw that he himself could change and could play a part in fighting for MRA. He thanked "the colleagues of the armies against which I bore arms in two world wars for receiving the Germans as brothers and equals." He added, "Here at Caux we have all tried in the spirit of Moral Re-Armament to bridge the differences which have divided us in the past and place in the forefront what shall unite us in the future. No one who believes in a future for himself, for his friends, neighbors, and children can escape from his responsibility to give his utmost for the security of every nation."

The results of this military conference at Caux were summed up by a group of generals, admirals, and senior air-force officers under four heads:

(1) A new understanding among some of the military leaders of the free countries of the total nature and scope of ideological war.

(2) A new appreciation of the need to win the cold war in the docks, factories, mines, and other sections of the home front.

(3) A new teamwork assured to the armed forces of many countries through the reconciliation of differences and the creation of strong personal links on a new ideological basis.

(4) A conviction among all concerned with defense that the ideology of Moral Re-Armament is the one uniting force in action capable of answering militant materialism on a world front.

Major-General de Vernejoul, who led the French Fifth Armored Division from the invasion of the south of France to the liberation of Alsace, gave his conclusions in one of the final sessions:

"Moral Re-Armament gives us tremendous hope because it provides a philosophy, a passion, and a plan adequate to turn back the tide of materialism. It is greater than the ideologies of materialism, and has the power to win their adherents. It will win not only in the West but behind the Iron Curtain as well."

In April 1951, the *Royal Air Force Quarterly* based its editorial on a study of this and other MRA conferences. Reviewing the urgent military situation and the need for immediate re-armament, the editorial states: "Before any material re-armament plan can succeed there must be a change of heart in our people; they must be convinced of the need for such action and the justice of the cause for which such arms would be used.

"Achieve this," the *Quarterly* continues, "and the nation will forego much that will otherwise be demanded; those in industry will not spare themselves in their united effort to produce armaments, the fighting forces will be provided with men enthusiastic in their military training and, should the need arise, 'believing in what they fight for and loving what they know,' they will face the enemy with the old unconquerable spirit.

"What we need is something to combat the spread of communist ideology in the minds of our people which is as dangerous, if not more dangerous, than the enormous military strength of Russia.

"The answer lies in developing moral re-armament alongside material re-armament. . . . The Moral Re-Armament organization is growing in strength and offers the very cause we need to reunite our people. Its principles are worthy of close study and our support. This growing ideology is practical. . . . It removes class distinction, industrial strife and all those things at the very root of our disunity.

"We recommend a study of moral re-armament by every officer and man in the Air forces. With a crew so united we could face with more equanimity the gathering storm."

Admiral Yngve Ekstrand, Commanding the Eastern Coast (Baltic Fleet), Sweden, said at the Washington Assembly in 1951, "Moral Re-Armament brings an idea into the heart of a soldier that he understands is worth fighting for, both against attacks from outside and inside, and it makes a soldier sensitive to subversive forces that are trying to attack his country. The armed forces are a great training ground where you can get your soldiers and the whole people trained, not only in military defense, but in ideological defense."

Admiral Ekstrand, as active commander of the fleet, fought publicly and boldly to make Moral Re-Armament the philosophy of nations. He traveled by air once to Riverside, California, and once to Washington, D.C., as delegate to Moral Re-Armament Assemblies.

He traveled to France, Britain, Denmark, Germany, and in other countries to speak and to work for MRA.

When he died suddenly, still on active service, in the spring of 1951, he was given a state funeral. The King and Queen of Sweden were represented, and public reference was made to his understanding of the ideological issues of our age.

II

The facts about Moral Re-Armament's war record speak for themselves.[18] Thousands of MRA-trained men served on every battlefront of the world in the last war. Many were decorated for gallantry. At MRA's London headquarters there is a large book containing the ribbons of the decorations won by Moral Re-Armament men in the British forces. They range from the Victoria Cross and the George Cross right through the list.

In America during the war Colonel Frank A. McHenry, executive officer of Morison Field, Florida, said of Moral Re-Armament, "I have never seen any group in uniform or out of it that is doing so much for the armed forces."

But valiant as was the service of Moral Re-Armament men in the armed forces, their unique contribution in the war years was in the field of ideology. Men in possession of the facts of this service evaluated it in its true perspective. Seen from the viewpoint of the Deputy Director of National Selective Service in America, Colonel John D. Langston, it was "the most effective medium through which Communism, Fascism and other totalitarian ideologies can be combated."

In a letter sent to Frank Buchman dated May 1948 and marked on the top "For Publication," Colonel Langston continues:

[18] See Document 18, "The War-time Program of MRA," from *The Army and Navy Journal*.

"The work of Moral Re-Armament has impressed me since 1941 when I had occasion to make some study of its scope and effectiveness in promoting better understanding between labor and management in industries essential to our national defense. The fact that such understanding was based on change of individuals through acceptance of Christ as the Composer of Conflicts between men, has been convincing that it will be effective in our conflict with totalitarian ideologies.

"Your work for the establishment of practical Christianity as the vital force in the defense of our democracy brought attack from the communistic press both during the war and since. Many patriotic citizens were misled by such attacks. I defended your work then. You have needed no defense since Communism has shown its continuing purpose to destroy or impair, if possible, all Christian institutions. I want you to know that it is my firm conviction that credence was never given by national leaders to attacks made on your group by communistic agents during the war. . . .

"As Chairman of the Presidential Appeals Board, and as Assistant Director of the Selective Service System during the war, I had absolute confidence in the patriotic endeavors of the Moral Re-Armament forces. I believe the millions of copies of *You Can Defend America* * distributed by Moral Re-Armament early in the war and subsequent work of the group aroused America to put forth its greatest effort to co-operate in necessary production for the armed forces and to keep solidified the defense of Democratic Ideals.

"I applaud your continuing efforts to revitalize the religious forces in the necessary fight to preserve civilization."

* *You Can Defend America* was a patriotic handbook with a foreword by General Pershing. The United States War Department Bureau of Public Relations termed it, "Probably the most challenging statement of this nation's philosophy of National Defense that has yet been written."

This MRA handbook was also endorsed by William Green, President, American Federation of Labor; Phillip Murray, President, Congress of Industrial Organizations; Howard Coonley, former President, National Association of Manufacturers; Brigadier General Monsignor William R. Arnold; Earl Godwin, widely known radio commentator and dean of White House correspondents; John W. Studebaker, U.S. Commissioner of Education; and Charles Edison, former Secretary of the Navy.

In another letter Colonel Langston states, "I have rejoiced over the fine work Moral Re-Armament has been doing to help beat back the tide of Communism. I believe you have the right weapon in this titanic battle."

Mr. H. Birchard Taylor, Vice-President of the Cramp Shipbuilding Company, building cruisers, destroyers, and submarines for the Navy, observed the results in the shipbuilding industry and said, "These men are worth a sizable task force to the Navy."

In the Lockheed Aircraft Plant in Los Angeles a nineteen-year-old shop steward, trained in Moral Re-Armament, was one of the 96,000 workers. He was elected to the central committee of his union. He built a team which thwarted the Communist attempt to capture the union. Throughout the whole of the war period there was not a single slowdown or strike. Bottlenecks were broken and production mounted. The president of the union speaking in Washington at the height of the war said, "There are planes on the war fronts today that would not be there but for the work of these men in Moral Re-Armament."

Today the young shop steward's work in the aircraft factories is carried on. His father recently received a letter from an official of his son's union, the International Association of Machinists, which says, "We have had considerable trouble with commie-liners distributing their literature at the Douglas Aircraft Company gates and also circulating the Stockholm Peace Petition. I wish to acknowledge thanks to MRA for the training that was extended to me, which was considerable, in coping with our situation in dealing with those supporters of the Communist Party at our gates."

III

In Canada Mr. Elliott Little, Director of the National Selective Service during the war, similarly recognized the essential contributions of Moral Re-Armament to the war effort.

He urged the Dominion Steel and Coal Corporation to obtain the help of MRA-trained men in dealing with a crisis in their mills and mines in Nova Scotia which produce twenty-five per cent of the steel and forty per cent of the coal of the dominion. To this bitter windswept coastal area of Canada's eastern provinces, where scarcely a tree breaks the monotony of the landscape, a hundred trained Communists had been sent to exploit the low morale of the men and to gain control. Production was down fifty per cent. Absenteeism ran as high as forty per cent. Mr. Little recognized that an increase in production of not more than five per cent would be worth fifty thousand men to Canada's war effort.

Sixty-six MRA-trained workers moved into the area, their campaign spearheaded by the revue, *Pull Together, Canada*. Within two months, thirty-three thousand people, workers and employers, had seen the play. An average of fifty calls a day had been made on key executives and workers. The MRA men had been down the mines and talked to the miners at the coalface. They had visited the dockyards and graving docks.

The effect of their campaign is typified by the change in one man, Bob Turnbull, president of the local miners' union and leader of a slowdown which had lasted six months.

Turnbull was known and feared as a bitter enemy of management; behind this lay problems in his home. He was the father of twelve children. His relationship with his wife was little happier than his attitude to management. It was symbolized by a simple domestic issue. Turnbull's wife wanted linoleum on the kitchen floor, but the money that might have bought the linoleum was being spent outside the home.

When an MRA worker went to stay in his home, Turnbull stopped spending on himself. With the money saved he bought his wife the linoleum. Change became a reality in Turnbull's life. Soon afterward a meeting was held in the miners' hall which was jammed not only with miners, but managers and superintendents. Everybody was waiting to hear what Turnbull would say, as he had never had the chance before to tell management exactly what he thought of them in front of his own crowd. When he stood up, he gave the audience the fireworks they had expected—but with a difference. He said, "As far as I am concerned I can offer no better appreciation of what I have heard about MRA than the promise to pull together wherever I am, first for the war, then for the peace." He spoke to the general manager on the spot, suggesting an informal committee of union members to lay before management specific proposals for increasing production.

Turnbull began to apply the principles of divine guidance to the question of how to solve the industrial crisis in Nova Scotia. He said to his own union men, "Every successful man plans his moves and writes out his plan. The working fellow is the only one who does not do it. Why don't we start and face ourselves and our problems squarely and write down the ideas we get? Then we'll keep the good ones and throw out the bad ones."

Soon after, there was a wildcat strike in No. 18 mine. Turnbull went to see the mine manager with whom he had a long-standing feud. His attitude was so different that the manager, instead of fighting him, promised a satisfactory answer to the men's demands if they went back to work. Turnbull went personally to see every member of the mine committee and a unanimous resolution was carried that the men go back.

Bob then invited the head of the mine committee with his wife to tea. They decided to have guidance together about how to handle the difficult mine manager when they went to see him in the morning. They got out pencils and paper and wrote down the thoughts which came to them.

The head of the mine committee wrote, "Meet the manager with a smile." His wife wrote, "Let him blow off first before you say anything to him." Two mornings later the headline in the paper read, "Satisfactory settlement reached in No. 18 dispute."

The manager called Turnbull into the office to thank him

for the way he had handled the affair and reported the whole matter to the district officials of the company.

This sort of story, multiplied throughout the mining communities, began to show results in the production charts. The manager of No. 11 Colliery estimated that loss of output due to absenteeism fell by eighty per cent in a three-month period.

The Caledonia Mine reported an increased output of three hundred tons a day of coal. The Princess Mine in the Sydney Mines, which used to average two stoppages a month, had no work stoppage of any kind in the months following the campaign of MRA. The president of one of the unions of the United Mine Workers of America in Cape Breton, who had been a prime mover in the slowdowns that reduced coal output from nineteen thousand to nine thousand tons a day, formed "Pull Together Committees" among his men. He began a series of conferences with other union officials and management, offering suggestions where different miners could be used with greater productive effect if they shifted jobs.

The Canadian Minister of Labor wired from Ottawa, "We need a new spirit of teamwork between labor and management if industry is to weather the difficult days that lie ahead. My department has received considerable evidence of the valuable contribution that the forces of Moral Re-Armament are making to produce this essential factor." The *Halifax Chronicle* said in an editorial, "Theirs is a contribution to the nation's fighting strength which cannot be overestimated." And the Ministry of Mines and Labor for Nova Scotia said that one hundred trained Communists who had been sent down to operate in the mines had been "completely neutralized" by the work of Moral Re-Armament.

Four years later the Lieutenant-Governor of Nova Scotia sent a message to Britain in which he said:

"*The Forgotten Factor* has the fundamental answer to deadlock. The ideologies now abroad in the world will wreck everything unless that white light of *The Forgotten Factor* guides us in dealing with them. It captured me and I long to see its message put at the heart of the wider issues that face the world today."

IV

In this age men with ideological training are the key personnel in every country. In peace or war the life of nations depends on them.

In peace it is their task to ensure that their own nation is proof against the assaults of alien ideologies which bid to capture it without a shot being fired, to unite a nation within itself and with other nations, to make peace permanent and rebuild the world.

If war comes, it is the distinctive service of these trained men to arm the nation with a fighting faith and so to safeguard the nation's factories, docks, and mines against systematic attempts at infiltration by false philosophies of materialism and pacifism; and to proclaim the mission of inspired democracy in such a way as to enlist the understanding and the backing of the world.

Today democracy must give priority to this factor and learn the secret of creating in every nation a strong force of trained personnel dedicated in peace or war to the winning of the millions.[32]

[32] See Document 32, "An Alternative."

IX. DESTINY OF EAST AND WEST

•

An ideology which can outbid ideologies of materialism must win the East as well as the West. It must have a prophetic conception of the destiny of the millions of Asia.

Asia has become an entity overnight. Composed of new political communities—Indonesia, India, Pakistan, Burma and now Communist China—she is very conscious of being Asia. Nationalism has achieved its aim. What is now to happen to the white-hot passions which carried nationalism to success?

Into this maelstrom has come a materialistic ideology. It has won China. It is penetrating every country in the East. Is it to be this ideology that will win this continent of ancient Faiths as it wakens to a new age?

The West, confronted with this situation, has concentrated on economic and technical aid. But is this adequate? Will economic aid succeed here where it failed in China, if the West is merely pouring in money while Russia and China pour in ideas?

The people of the East show little eagerness to adopt the views of the West. Pandit Nehru made that clear again during the Korean crisis. In an earlier speech he gave a useful hint. The West, he said, must win the heart of the East.

At a recent parliamentary conference in Dublin, delegates from the United States were shocked at the bitterness which the representatives of Asia expressed toward white people. For hundreds of years white people have adopted an attitude of effortless superiority toward the teeming millions of the

East. Now these millions, industrially and ideologically awakening, resent it.

Typical of the Western attitude are the words of a European prime minister who, referring to an Eastern visitor, said, "They should never have been given independence. They have been fighting among themselves ever since. They are not fit for it."

A Burmese woman, to whom this conversation was repeated, replied with a smile, "And are the European nations fit to govern themselves? *They* have killed millions of men in two world wars in my lifetime. So let us not criticize each other, East and West, but let us learn new things together."

I

The name of this woman is Ma Nyein Tha. She is known as the most widely traveled Burmese woman. She is playing a key part in the fight for unity between East and West.

She has talked with a king of England in private audience at Buckingham Palace. She squatted on the floor of Mahatma Gandhi's hut. She made such an impression on Gandhi that he afterward said to a friend, "Ma Nyein Tha, I fell in love with her." She has stayed in the homes of miners in the Ruhr and of workers in the East End of London. She has broadcast to the world from Britain and America. Thirty thousand people listened to her, among others, at the Hollywood Bowl. A Turkish newspaper recently described her as "the wisest woman in Asia."

Ma Nyein Tha was at twenty-one the headmistress in a school of 650 girls in Burma. It is the oldest and most famous girls' school of that country. She was so efficient and so remote. "Just like parts of the British administration in Burma," she says with a chuckle. Then one day some of the girls rebelled and wrote to the newspapers a long list of grievances.

She was not only angry. She was hurt inside, because she loved her work and thought she was doing it ably. So she ran away. She went to Rangoon. "God spoke to my heart in Rangoon about those girls," she says. "I began to face the fact that I hated them. I saw that when I became headmistress of the school my head had grown very big. When your head grows big, your heart grows small." So Ma Nyein Tha went back to the school and apologized to the girls. Much to her astonishment, the girls—and some of the teachers too—told her how frightened of her they had been. They had never dared to tell her that before. They became united.

Ma Nyein Tha began to understand the importance of absolute moral standards. With standards of relative love and honesty, she and her school were divided and distrusted each other. With absolute love and honesty coming in, unity followed. What was true of a school could go through a nation. That has been her message to the world ever since.

At Caux in September 1950, Ma Nyein Tha with her musical voice, a flower set in the high crown of her jet-black hair, her eyes eager, and her fingers full of movement to explain each point, told the delegates from all over the world, "I am not interested in moderate standards. Who wants an egg for breakfast that is moderately fresh? Or to live in a house that keeps out most of the water? Or how would you like to be in a boat that floats most of the time? Or to draw almost all of your salary? Honesty, purity, unselfishness, and love, these are the standards of Moral Re-Armament. And they are absolute. One hundred per cent. People are like tables with four legs. It's the same with moral standards. If one leg is a bit shorter than the other three, the table wobbles when anyone touches it. It's all right to look at. But it's not safe to use. If you put a lamp on it, it may fall down and burn up the house.

"What happens when we live according to absolute moral standards?" continued Ma Nyein Tha. "We are like a pool of water, clear, cool, and sparkling, where everyone drinks and finds new life. Then a little leaf falls in, a stone falls in, a thorn falls in, a twig falls in, and they all go down to the bottom. Somebody stirs the pool, and you cannot drink the water.

But clear the whole thing out. Throw the leaf away. Throw the stone away. Throw the thorn away. Throw the twig away. Then, when somebody comes and stirs it, there is nothing to come up. The pool remains clear and sparkling. Anyone can drink it and get fresh life. That is the clearing out we need all the time."

When Ma Nyein Tha was invited to broadcast to the whole of Burma on their National Day, she said, "What is the answer to all this dishonesty, anyway? The answer to dishonesty is—an honest man. I would like to see honesty walking around on two feet. May I remind you—all of you have two feet?" Then she added, "The trouble with us is that we are an individualistic people. Look at the word. Five 'I's' and one 'U.' Look at the word Unity. One 'U' and one 'I,' and the 'U' comes first.

"If I point my finger at someone else," added Ma Nyein Tha, suiting the action to the word, "there are *three* fingers pointing back at me."

Ma Nyein Tha began to join in a fight for a remade Burma. In Burma ninety per cent of the people live in agricultural villages, just as they do in China, India, and Russia. In all such countries an ideology to be adequate must work in the village communities. An Englishman who had been gripped by Moral Re-Armament went to one of the areas of Burma where the population is divided between the Burmese and Karen communities but also included Chinese and Indians, Hindus, Moslems, Christians, and Buddhists. When he was honest with the villagers, the villagers began to be honest with him. Men began to learn the secret of changing and bringing change to others.

Let Ma Nyein Tha tell the story of the buffaloes. "One of the men in the village lost his buffalo. That is serious in Burma. He could not plow the land without his buffalo. What was he to do? We say in Burma, 'If you lose a thing once, you go to hell ten times,' because you keep on accusing everyone else of having stolen it. But the people of this village had learned to listen to God. The thought came to them to go to a nearby village and cook their evening meal under the big tree in the middle of the village street. So they went and cooked their rice and curry. Presently the villagers came back from their work in the fields and began to ask each other, 'Who are those strangers under our tree?' They sat around. Nothing was said about the missing buffalo. But the visitors began to tell them how they were learning to live absolute honesty. When you have an experience to share, it comes from your heart and goes into other people's hearts. It is not a point of view to air, but reality to share. Soon the visitors saw a group of men get up and disappear. They were worried because the village they were in was a very notorious village. But the men came back and said, "Look here. Perhaps you have lost a buffalo? Well, we took it. But we cannot give it back because we have eaten it." They offered to pay for it. The owner said sixty rupees would be the price. Then the thieves insisted on paying eighty rupees. So they used the extra twenty rupees to have a thanksgiving feast all together.

"You see," concludes Ma Nyein Tha, "the villagers, instead of getting up against each other as some nations and races and classes do, listened to the great wisdom of not who was right but what was right, and what they should do about it. So they became friends and became united."

The spirit of that village community spread throughout an entire area. A government official responsible for the area was told by the head men of the villages, "We want to stop giving bribes." The government official had done quite well out of the system of corruption, which is one of Burma's greatest problems. His tactful reply was, "If you don't offer bribes, nobody can take them."

One result is that the cost of a license to fell timber has been cut down to one-twentieth of what it was under the system of bribery.

When the Japanese invaded Burma, civil war and massacre broke out in many places, but here there was peace. In the whole area, where previously the inhabitants had stolen from each other and often killed each other, a plan was made, in the face of Japanese confiscation of supplies, to conserve and share what was available.

General Aung San, when Chief Executive under the British government, traveled thirty hours to see for himself this demonstration of an ideology at work. Twenty thousand people of the area had gathered at the village for an MRA Assembly. "This is what I want for the whole country," he said. When Aung San and seven members of his cabinet were assassinated, Mrs. Aung San was given cabinet rank. She came to the Whitsun gathering for Moral Re-Armament at Gelsenkirchen in June 1950. There she said, "My husband and I have seen the areas in Burma where MRA is at work. It has brought unity. Our present Prime Minister, Thakin Nu,[19] wants honesty and unity too. We need MRA to help us reach this goal."

Thakin Nu visited London himself in 1950. He came for the memorial service in Westminster Abbey to the soldiers who fell in the Burma campaign. He came at the suggestion of Ma Nyein Tha's friend, the Englishman who first carried an answer to the villages of Burma—George West, Bishop of Rangoon.

At a dinner given to him by the Burmese community in London, during his visit, the Prime Minister told them, "Live a life of honesty in Britain so that you are true ambassadors of your nation. And live in unity with the British."

He paid his third visit to Frank Buchman's home and in his speech of thanks said, "You find here a warmth and understanding you find nowhere else in the West."

In 1951 Mahn Ba Saing, Minister for Karen Affairs in the Government of Burma, went to the National Assembly of MRA held at Washington. He went with the approval of Thakin Nu. On his return he submitted a report to his col-

[19] Thakin Nu sent a message to Frank Buchman at the Caux Assembly in 1949. See Document 19, "The First Objective."

leagues in the Cabinet. This is what he said. "Moral Re-Armament has been tried and tested and found successful in country after country. We realize how necessary it is to solve the refugee problem, to bring to an end the conflict with the insurgents and to stabilize the economic life of the country. We realize only too well that, unless we solve these problems, and that soon, we may well be overcome by the threats to our freedom and our future."

Mahn Ba Saing proposed three things. First, that Burma should follow the example of India and invite Dr. Buchman to bring an international force to Burma. Second, that Burma should send a picked delegation to the next MRA Assembly. And third that "As Moral Re-Armament teaches, we should start with ourselves in applying the standards of absolute honesty, absolute purity, absolute unselfishness, and absolute love to our own lives, homes, and national situations."

II

The first big impact of MRA on India began when a British Government official decided that the best way he could win the hearts of the East was to admit that he had been cold and superior to his Indian colleagues and subordinates, and apologized to them for his attitude. The effect of this was startling. The Indians said they had never believed a white man could say "Sorry" with such frankness. The life of that community began to be transformed.

Mahatma Gandhi heard the news of this remarkable Englishman in his ashram. He did not believe it could be true. Some months later he said to his informant, "I had that story investigated. It is *all* true." Gandhi described Moral Re-Armament as "the best thing that has come out of the West."

Since the war Caux has been a magnet for the leadership of India. Among the first to come was Ragunath Nimbkar, one of the pioneers of Communism in that vast sub-continent. Nimbkar's earliest memories were of an endless struggle against debt in a small village near Bombay, while the merchants and the British lived in what seemed to him luxury in the big city. His parents scraped to send him to college. But the boy had already flung himself so violently into endless bitter political activity that he failed his examinations.

In 1922 he was sent to jail for the first time. The Communists got in touch with Nimbkar when he came out of prison and he became a founder-member of the All-India Communist Party.

By 1933 the Communists were ready for a trial of strength. But in Calcutta the plot was discovered. Nimbkar was the chief of the accused in the famous "Meerut Conspiracy Case" and was given the heaviest sentence, twelve years' imprisonment. This later was reduced to one year—twelve months of fanatical brooding and bitterness behind bars.

In 1939 he was elected Workers' Delegate to the ILO Conference in Geneva. From there he traveled to Moscow. There he was shown to a magnificent room overlooking the Red Square. But at the last moment a more privileged guest arrived and Nimbkar was given a less good room. He was deeply hurt. He returned from Moscow disillusioned with the Party but still in love with its idea.

In 1941 the British put him in jail again because of his hostility to the "Imperialist war." One year later he and other Communists were released to win the support of Indian workers for the war effort which now had Soviet blessing. He was made Labor Welfare Adviser to the Government.

In 1944 he was appointed by the government to represent labor at a committee of inquiry in connection with a threatened postal strike in Bombay. He found that the president of the committee, Krishna Prasada, then Postmaster General of Bombay, had invited the six members of the committee to his home. It was a new home and this was the housewarming. Krishna Prasada is an old friend of Frank Buchman and of Moral Re-Armament.

Nimbkar found himself in a varied gathering. There was

Sir Francis Low, editor of the *Times of India*, Lionel Jardine, British Resident (Senior Civil Service Officer) at Baroda, the man whose change of attitude had so excited the interest of Mahatma Gandhi; a cotton magnate from Egypt; a smart young British Captain, ADC to the Governor of Bombay, and others.

Nimbkar was suspicious. He announced baldly, "I am only interested in a tangible solution to the working conditions of the postal servant." Nobody argued. The British Resident simply said that in the past his attitude had been indifferent, superior and wrong toward Indians, and that he had had to change.

The Postmaster General said he was sorry he had not taken trouble to be fully informed what the workers' wages were and how they related to the cost of living. At which the cotton manufacturer described how in Egypt he had learned to put all his cards on the table with his workers and give as much care to his workers' wages as to his own salary. Nimbkar's key Marxist argument—that a person will only change when the system changes—broke down before this first-hand evidence. He had never believed that change could come by choice instead of by violent action.

So the following day Nimbkar, the agitator, presented himself at the Taj Mahal Hotel where the Englishman was staying. The fire and bitterness of a lifetime poured out of him. He attacked the Englishman savagely. "After 150 years of British rule is there such poverty in the world as in India? You retire on fat pensions for which we, the underfed, have to pay. You take millions out of the country. Then you come and talk to us about Moral Re-Armament. We are a religious people. It is not *we* who need to be different."

A dozen points of self-justification leapt into Jardine's mind. But he did not hit back. He simply said that the British people like himself had made many mistakes, but his aim now was to see things different for the future.

Nimbkar's rage drained away in the face of such disarming honesty. But he was still skeptical.

The test and proof for him came in Krishna Prasada's handling of the Post Office crisis. It began with deadlock between government and trade unions, and ended with unanimous agreement which raised the wages of twenty thousand lower-paid postal workers and affected indirectly the pay of eighty thousand more postal employees in other provinces.

That a committee consisting of five heterogeneous members and representing conflicting interests could produce a unanimous report was considered to be a miracle; indeed, there had been forebodings that there would be three or four separate reports.

Nimbkar returned to Delhi. He was in favor of the principles of MRA, but not yet a master of its practice. He had a serious quarrel with his chief, Dr. Ambedkar, leader of the sixty million Untouchables, and resigned his post. Then he was caught up in a textile dispute involving five thousand workers and to dramatize the situation went on a nineteen-day hunger strike. In the middle of his fast he was amazed to receive a warm letter asking after his well-being from an English friend of Jardine's. Later Nimbkar said, "This gesture in a time of trouble meant more to me than all the arguments."

He was invited to Caux and, after consulting with Mahatma Gandhi, who approved and asked for a report when he got back to India, he accepted. His visit to Caux was the turning point of his life. Before he left he said, "A few years ago I hated one and all except the workers of the world. I hated the British imperialists bitterly. I have been very moved here to meet Britishers who admit mistakes and have changed. I want to shake hands and say that when India and England work together, it will be a great force for remaking the world."

He sent a letter to Dr. Ambedkar apologizing for the anger and self-will which had led to his resignation as Labor Welfare Adviser. This letter moved Dr. Ambedkar profoundly.

By the time he got back to India communal bitterness had

flared up. Nimbkar told the press, "This communal situation plays into the hands of the enemies of India's freedom. MRA stands for a third way in such disputes."

Early in 1947 he became chairman of a committee of inquiry into labor wages and conditions. In April 1948, he completed a report which was unanimously signed by workers' and employers' representatives—although it recommended considerable sacrifice for the employers.

The trade union leader, Mr. B. K. Mukerjee, explains this unanimity which startled Indian opinion, "The force of his conviction changed everyone around him."

And until his death in 1948, Nimbkar the Communist pioneer fought to get Marxists and management to Caux, as both, he felt, needed the power of the greater ideology that had captured his own life.

The Deputy Chairman of the National Planning Commission, of which Pandit Nehru is chairman, said, "Here is a force that can change selfishness and greed and all that is wrecking the souls of people. Until I met MRA I had not felt confident that there was an idea which could be applied universally as an adequate answer.

An interesting sign of new unity between the peoples of the East and West came at Caux in 1950 when the Independence Days of Pakistan [20] and India were celebrated.

The new flags were hoisted before the entire Assembly by a Moslem, who had had to leave all his possessions when India was given the district where he lived; a Hindu revolutionary leader, who had had a price on his head; and an English officer, who had tried to track him down, but only caught up with him at Caux.

[20] Among Pakistan leaders who have been at Caux are the Hon. Malik Mohammed Anwar Khan, Political Adviser to the Governor of the Punjab; Major-General S.M.A. Faruki; Commodore Hajee Mohammed Siddiq Choudri, Chief of Staff, Royal Pakistan Navy; and Mr. Zahur Ahmed, President of the Chamber of Commerce, Lahore.

See Document 20, "Greater History" by the Prime Minister of East Pakistan.

Those who saw this scene remembered the words of Mr. Jinnah during an evening of his last visit to London which he spent with Moral Re-Armament. He came tense and weary, but as time went on he relaxed and talked in a way which some of his colleagues declared they had never heard before. And as he left he said, "You have the answer to the hates of the world here."

III

Remembering Mr. Nehru's words about the West winning the heart of the East, it is worth quoting from the letter [21] received by Frank Buchman in September 1950 from leaders in India who have met him personally or known his work. Among the signatories are the Deputy Chairman and three members of the National Planning Commission, the President of the National Trades Union Congress, the Vice-Chancellor of Madras University, the Chief Minister of West Bengal, the Minister of Education for the United Provinces, the Minister of Labor for Bihar, and the Chairman of Tata Industries.

"We are convinced that the true hope for bringing lasting change in social and economic conditions and for bringing peace to the world lies in multiplying such practical results as we believe to have been achieved by Moral Re-Armament.

[21] See Document 21, "From Crisis to Cure."

The following members of the Invitation Committee have visited the World Assembly for Moral Re-Armament at Caux: Dr. S. N. Agarwal, Secretary, Foreign Department Sarvodaya Samaj, Wardha; the late Sir Gurunath Bewoor, Managing Director, Air India, Ltd.; Shri Khandubhai Desai, President of the Indian National Trades Union Congress; Sir Lakhshmanaswami Mudaliar, Vice-Chancellor, Madras University; Shri Gulzarilal Nanda, Deputy Chairman, National Planning Commission; Shri Ramnath Podar, industrialist; Shri Krishna Prasada, Director General, Posts and Telegraphs; Sir Sri Ram, Former Chairman of the Indian Chamber of Commerce; the Hon. Dr. B. C. Roy, Chief Minister, West Bengal; The Hon. A. N. Sinha, Minister of Labor, Bihar.

Indian trade-union leaders at Caux have numbered seventeen, including thirteen presidents, vice-presidents, secretaries, and members of executive committees of National Trade Unions.

Industrialists include four directors of Tata Industries.

. . . We consider that such moral re-armament of the nations is the need of the hour and the hope of the future. . . . We would like you to know how glad we would all be to see you in India this winter along with an international team so that we may profit by your experience. . . . Together we must succeed in turning the world from crisis to cure, and in demonstrating an overarching ideology for management and labor, for Left and Right, for East and West."

X. "ALL ASIA WILL LISTEN"

•

Lenin thought and spoke in terms of ideology. He once indicated that the shortest way from the Kremlin to the White House and No. 10 Downing Street lay through Peking and Calcutta.

Events in the East prove the force of his theories. Russia has shaken Washington and London by her advances in Asia, and her penetration there sets the pace in the world today.

How can the statesmen of the free world recapture the initiative in Asia?

How, for instance, can the ideological vacuum in Japan be filled? Overwhelming defeat in battle has given that country a new constitution. The framework of democratic society is being inserted into the life of those islands. But a few miles away are the coasts of Russia and China and the idea which is dominating the lives of their millions has long since crossed the narrow waters between. So the way Japan will go has yet to be decided by her eighty million people.

I

In Washington, on July 28, 1950, a little less than five years after the atom bombs fell on Hiroshima and Nagasaki and nine years after Pearl Harbor, a remarkable event took place. For the first time in the history of the United States, spokesmen for Japan addressed the two Houses of Congress.

They were leaders of a delegation of seventy-six Japanese who had flown across the world to Caux and were now on their way back to Tokyo.

Senator H. Alexander Smith of New Jersey escorted six members of the Japanese Diet, who were part of the delegation, onto the floor of the Senate. The rest of the party occupied a section of the gallery.

The Vice-President of the United States, Mr. Alben Barkley, introduced the visitors. Then Senator Connally, Chairman of the Foreign Affairs Committee, rose. In the course of his speech he said, "I pray God that the people of Japan, like the people of America, will want peace and will strive for it. . . . We welcome you. We wish your country well. We hope you can rehabilitate your broken enterprises and turn them all into the pathway of co-operation and peace in behalf of all the peoples of the world."

Mr. Kuriyama, representing the Japanese Prime Minister's party, replied. Mr. Kuriyama's speech was interrupted no fewer than seven times by loud applause, not only from the floor of the Chamber but also from the galleries. The Senators rose to him as he finished his speech. He said, "We went to Caux in search of the true content of democracy. We found the ideology which will feed democracy in Japan and which at the same time is the powerful answer to Communism." Then, after expressing gratitude for America's forgiveness and her aid in helping Japanese recovery, Mr. Kuriyama continued, "We are sincerely sorry for Japan's big mistake. We broke almost a century-old friendship between the two countries." The Senate and the galleries sat in dead silence, deeply moved by this honest apology from another nation.

The delegation was welcomed with equal warmth in the House of Representatives.

Speaker Rayburn said, "To say that these distinguished visitors from Japan are welcome here is putting it very mildly. . . . It gives us the opportunity of showing you that in the future we want to be your friends."

Minority Leader Martin also joined in the welcome. He said, "We want to make Japan one of the great countries of the world, a country that will join with us and the other forces that will fight for freedom and for better days for peoples everywhere. . . . The peoples of our two great countries working together can be a positive force—a positive force for better things for all the people of the world."

Mr. Kitamura, the Secretary General of the Democratic Party and former Finance Minister, was the spokesman for the Japanese. He said, "We, the Japanese people, feel responsible for finding an answer to Communism, an answer that will give a basis on which inspired democracy can be established in the Far East." He then said that the Japanese delegates had found this answer at Caux. After the war Japan had thought that her most urgent need was economic rehabilitation. A far more basic reconstruction was needed and they had discovered in Moral Re-Armament the moral basis on which alone a true economic order could be established.

The State Department gave a reception for the Japanese at Prospect House, where they met John Foster Dulles, the State Department adviser, who is responsible for the Japanese treaty.

The New York Times commented on these developments in an editorial of July 29, 1950: "It is sadly true, among nations as among individuals, that the friends of yesterday are not always the friends of today. In compensation, the enemies of yesterday may not be enemies today. . . . Peace and goodwill can return, even after the most terrible events. The Mayors of Hiroshima and Nagasaki were among yesterday's visitors. If they felt that they too had something to forgive they had achieved that miracle. For a moment one could see out of the present darkness into the years when all men may be brothers." [22]

The *Saturday Evening Post* commented in an editorial, "Mr. Kuriyama's statement would be hard for an American to understand. (Yet) the idea of a nation admitting that it could be mistaken has a refreshing impact. . . . Perhaps even Americans could think up a few past occasions of which it could safely be said, 'We certainly fouled things up that time.' "

[22] See Document 22, "Enemies Become Friends."

On the fifth anniversary of the atom bombing of Hiroshima, members of a Japanese delegation broadcast in Los Angeles from coast to coast on the Columbia Broadcasting System. Governor Earl Warren of California and Mayor Fletcher Bowron of Los Angeles spoke on the same program with them.

II

How did these historic events happen? In 1949 the first major Japanese delegation to Europe since the war traveled to Caux, with the sanction of General MacArthur. They numbered thirty-four and were led by Mr. Tetsu Katayama, first elected post-war Prime Minister of Japan and head of the Social Democratic Party.*

At the suggestion of some of Mr. Katayama's delegation, two MRA workers spent the spring of 1950 in Japan. They traveled from city to city, leaving behind them MRA cells in the factories and communities. They discovered people who, all through the difficult years of militaristic dictatorship and war, had kept the flame of MRA alight in Japan.

The response to their message was amazing. Within a few months seventy-six leaders of Japanese life had been so captured by it that they were ready to leave their official desks, their trade union activities, and their civic responsibilities and travel halfway round the world, paying their own expenses, to find an ideological answer for their nation.

III

This later delegation is said to be the largest and most representative group of political, industrial, and civic leaders to

* Other members of the delegation included Mr. Kensuke Horinouchi, former Ambassador to Washington, who was withdrawn shortly before Pearl Harbor on account of his opposition to Japan's military aims; Mr. Tokutaro Kitamura, Secretary General of the Democratic Party and former Minister of Finance; Mr. S. Yamada, M.P. for Hiroshima; Dr. Ayusawa, Executive Director of the Central Labor Relations Board; and editorial representatives of the newspapers *Asahi* and *Mainichi*, which have a combined circulation of seven million.

leave Japan since the war. It included the governors of seven prefectures; members of the Democratic, Liberal, and Socialist parties in both Houses of Parliament; the Mayors of Hiroshima, Nagasaki, Kobe, and Nagano; the president of the largest electrical company (Shibaura Electric) and of the largest insurance company (Nippon Life); trades union leaders; and leading educational, press, and radio personalities.

Before they left, a farewell luncheon was given them by the Prime Minister. Mr. Yoshida told them, "In 1870 a representative group of Japanese traveled to the West. On their return they changed the course of Japanese life. I believe that when this delegation returns, you, too, will open a new page in our history.[23]

The Japanese traveled through Switzerland, Germany, France, and Britain and visited the United States on their way back to Tokyo. They spent three weeks at Caux, mingling with statesmen and industrial leaders from both the victorious and the conquered nations.

In Germany, the United States High Commissioner received them in his Bonn residence. The Chancellor of the Federal Republic, Dr. Konrad Adenauer, when he gave them an official welcome, said that he knew Caux well, and much appreciated Dr. Buchman's great contribution to international unity and social justice.*

A party of eleven flew to Berlin at the invitation of the Lord Mayor, Professor Ernst Reuter. The Mayor of Hiroshima, Mr. Shinzo Hamai, presented Reuter with a cross carved from the wood of a four-hundred-year-old tree planted at the time of the foundation of the city. This tree was a sacred camphor tree. Its roots ran under roads and pavements which rolled in waves over them. For no man would cut the

---

[23] See Document 23, "Foundation of a Nation."

* The Federal Vice-Chancellor, Mr. Blücher, together with Mr. Wildermuth, Minister of Reconstruction, Dr. Lukaschek, Minister for Refugees, and Mr. Storch, Minister of Labor, gave a dinner to the Japanese delegation. Other receptions were given by the Lord Mayors of Berlin, Cologne, Duisburg, Düsseldorf, Essen, Gelsenkirchen, Hamburg, and Bremen.

root of the sacred tree. The tree was disintegrated by the atomic bomb, but its heart stood firm. From this heart the cross was cut. The smell of the camphor still lingers in it.

Meanwhile, another group visited Rome, where they were received by the Pope and by members of the Italian Government. The whole party also visited Paris and London, where they were given official receptions by civic and political authorities.

IV

During their world mission the Japanese began to pattern in their own delegation the secret of unity for their nation. One of the delegates was Mr. Eiji Suzuki, the chief of police of Osaka. His work is dangerous. His wife said that she never knows when he leaves home in the morning whether he will get safely back at night, so violent is the hatred that his work has aroused in the hearts of some of the people of Osaka.

He is a big man, with a mask of toughness which his job demands. One of his bitter enemies was another member of the delegation, Mr. Katsuji Nakajima, a leader of the two hundred thousand strong Metalworkers' Union of Japan.

Mr. Nakajima is little more than half the size of the chief of police, but full of fight. He was in Hiroshima when the bomb fell and bears the marks of it to this day. He is a devoted husband and father, and in his spare time paints and draws with beauty.

But he loathed the chief of police so much that all the way across the world in the airplane he would not speak to him.

His eyes spark with fire behind his spectacles. But the water of tears quenched the fire as he went to see the chief of police one day at Caux and begged pardon for his hate. He told him he realized that all his talk of the brotherhood of man was unreal when he had so burning a hate for another man.

Next day the chief of police rose from his seat in a session of the Assembly and before fourteen hundred people from nations all over the world begged the pardon of Mr. Nakajima for his hatred of the Socialists and Communists. He said, "I have been overcome by your tremendous spirit. There has been a chain reaction in my own heart. Although I am opposed to Communism, I have lost completely my hatred of the Communists whom I have blamed and fought for years."

Someone from another country, who had lived for years in Japan and knows the great reserve and proper pride of her people, said that if he had not seen this with his own eyes he would never have believed it possible. One of the members of the Japanese Diet described it as "the greatest gift that could be given to Japan. It answers the hatred that threatens to tear Japan with civil war."

Nakajima and the chief of police decided to fight together to carry the answer to hatred and the secret of unity to the whole of the East.

In a farewell speech before leaving America on August 6, 1950—fifth anniversary of the dropping of the atom bomb on Hiroshima—Mr. Nakajima said, "I had used as my only weapon in the labor movement the weapon of hatred. I went to Caux with hatred of the Americans and capitalists as the basis of the philosophy which I fed to union members. But there I began to realize that in this conflict of hate I could not solve the problems of my family nor the problems within my own heart nor the problems of my comrades in Labor. The experience of removing this hate was to me an even greater spiritual shock than the physical shock I received at Hiroshima. This is the only road for Japan and the only road for the world. Words are catching in my throat. I do not know just exactly what to say. But I am going to leave tomorrow with the strong faith that our hearts will all be tied together. As I arrive in Japan there will be many friends waiting for me, among them my friends in the Communist Party. These Communist friends will be asking many, many questions—for example, what I saw in U.S.A. I intend to answer them in this way, 'Japan and America must be tied together. But how can they be tied together? The Japanese must change now. But undoubtedly the Americans will have to change a bit too. A new ideology will bring together Japan and America. Change and unity—these are the things that will bring real peace to the world.' In our corner of the Orient, blood is being spilled. But don't forget some of us will also be fighting with everything we have for a new ideology."

In the first three months after their return members of the delegation have spoken to over a million people in meetings, and through the press and radio. They have also demonstrated in their new-found teamwork the unity which an overarching ideology can produce. Conservatives and Socialists have been working and speaking together. Public apologies and reconciliations have given clear evidence of the determination of these men to apply their convictions.

Suzuki, the chief of police, is doing all he can to change the 3,500,000 citizens of Osaka. The four standards of Moral Re-Armament are on the wall of every police box in the city. He apologized publicly to the Speaker of the Osaka Prefectural Assembly, who was suing him in the law courts, for the bitterness he had harbored against him. The Speaker arose and apologized in his turn for having maliciously attacked Suzuki and his wife. The lawsuit was withdrawn. This public reconciliation created a sensation throughout the city. The newspapers wrote: "The Chief of Police has changed 180 degrees."

His men felt the difference, too. The Precinct Head of Juvenile Crime Detection had divorced his wife. He was so astounded by the change in Suzuki that he asked him what had happened to him. Facing the challenge of absolute moral standards, he went to his wife and mother-in-law and said he had been wrong. His wife forgave him and they are reunited "with open hearts to each other and bright hopes for the future," to quote the man's own words.

Nakajima has spoken with such effect about the change in his own life which an idea superior to Communism has brought, and about the barrenness of mere anti-Communism, that he has been invited no less than three times to speak publicly and train the citizens of the reddest section of Nagano in MRA.

Nakajima also reports that in his mountainous and beautiful province of Nagano, which is called "the roof of Japan," MRA has penetrated even to the remotest mountain villages. Many of these villages have been dominated by Communism, but the biggest crowds ever seen there gather to meet Nakajima and his friends in MRA. Already a new spirit is at work, and spreading fast. In Nagano Prefecture, says Nakajima, there used to be twenty-four elected officials who were Communists, but in the recent election not one of them was re-elected. The Governor of the Prefecture and the Mayor of the city were both at Caux, both fought for Moral Re-Armament, and both were re-elected.

And Suzuki, the chief of police, writes, "Two things seem to impress people most—one being my experience of change at Caux and the other the practice of the highest ideology in the world. I am firmly determined to extend MRA in Japan for the rehabilitation of this country."

v

The Japanese summed up the potential significance of their journey for the whole of Asia in a statement [24] which appeared on the front page of *The London Observer*. They said, "Russia has advanced in Asia because the Soviet Government understands the art of ideological war. It fights for the minds of men. We appeal to the governments and peoples of the West to do the same—to make themselves expert in the philosophy and practice of Moral Re-Armament, which is the ideology of the future. Then all Asia will listen."

[24] See Document 24, "All Asia Will Listen."

XI. AFRICA WILL CHOOSE

•

One hundred and fifty million Africans live on this continent. For three centuries the slave-ships came there and the traders with whips and chains loaded their cargoes and dragged them across the world. For nearly a hundred years they have lived under the domination of European countries.

For more than one hundred years, the Africans have seen gold, diamonds, timber, palm oil, and wealth of every kind pouring from their native land. The Africans have provided the manpower, and the traders and settlers from Europe have amassed the riches.

Notwithstanding the many benefits of Western "civiliza-tion"—administration, law and order, health and education, and the devoted service of many Europeans who have given the best years of their lives there—the African feels that he would be better off managing his own affairs. The dream and the dominant passion among those Africans who are now wakening to world events is *Self-Government*.

The materialism of the Western world they know and hate. The materialistic ideology from Eastern Europe has not yet captured them. But, as something which may help them to break the power of those who govern and, they believe, ex-ploit them, the Africans tend to welcome Communism. Cer-tainly few things irritate an African more than having "the danger of Communism" pointed out to him by a member of an "imperialist race."

At the same time they are in a dilemma and have not yet

decided where to turn. Their reason tells them their security and destiny lie with the democracies of the West. Their emotions urge them toward Eastern Communism.

But when Africans see an ideology at work which fights for both East and West, an ideology based on change for the white people as well as for every other race, they accept it wholeheartedly.

I

A large section of the white race on this continent live in the Union of South Africa. How is the ideology of change affecting the Afrikaans and British people there and their relationship to each other and to the colored races?

Through 1949 and 1950 *The Forgotten Factor* has been presented in South Africa. There have been 104 performances seen by seventy-five thousand people. Half the Cabinet and more than half of Parliament have attended.

Three meetings have been held in the Houses of Parliament. One was chaired by the Hon. C. M. van Coller, then Speaker of the House of Assembly, one by the Hon. J. F. T. Naudé, the present Speaker.[25] Mr. Naudé sent a personal notice to every member of the House. The third was chaired by the Hon. C. A. van Niekerk, President of the Senate.

Following these meetings four members of the South African Parliament flew to Caux. Two were from the United Party, one from the Afrikaner Party, and one was a Nationalist. After Caux some of them toured Germany, Holland, and Britain to see MRA in action. The Nationalist Member addressed a gathering of businessmen in London in these words:

"It is surprising to be welcomed into a British gathering in this way. It is evidence of something new, as I have been fighting the British all my life. My fathers did before me. In school I had been forced to learn English, but at home I had been taught to hate. My children I taught to hate too.

[25] See Document 25, "The Greatest of Memories."

"I saw a lot at Caux. Then I went to Germany and Holland. I stayed in private houses and discussed things privately with people. I spent an evening in the home of the manager of the Gelsenkirchen Coal Company. I saw his wife, a cultured lady, entertain with open heart a Communist trade union leader from her husband's mines. I myself was anti-Communist, but I spent one of the happiest evenings of my life in the home of a former Communist.

"If we in South Africa want to save ourselves we must look across the seas. Our frontier is not on the Limpopo but where the last man in this world is."

Performances of *The Forgotten Factor* were seen by all sections of South African life, European, native, colored people of the Cape, Indian. The first performance for a wholly native audience was in one of the townships on the Gold Reef. Here audiences had a habit of coming late to the theater. But twenty minutes before curtain time the hall was so crowded that not one more could possibly get in. At the end of the performances the audience rose and sang with deep feeling the Zulu national anthem.

Other performances for native audiences were held throughout the industrial centers, as well as at Adams College in Natal and at Fort Hare. "One reason we Bantus do not get further is that we do not agree among ourselves," explained one of them. "If a Zulu is chairman of a council the Basutos will not co-operate, and if a Basuto is chairman the Zulus walk out. Since we saw *The Forgotten Factor* we have had the best meeting of our Township Council ever." One of the Bantu leaders said, "This is melting people's hearts, and that is what we need most of all in this country."

Race conflict is near the surface in South Africa. There has been loss of life this past year. But on some occasions where trouble was expected none occurred, and more than one official in native affairs claims that *The Forgotten Factor* has been instrumental in averting bloodshed.

Manilal Gandhi, who edits the African paper *Indian Opin-*

ion, which his father Mahatma Gandhi founded, came with his family. Describing the play in his paper he said, "Moral Re-Armament is a lighthouse in this dark and stormy world of ours, and it will guide us to the right way. We feel that the darkness that surrounded our hearts has been lifted." This performance was in the Gandhi Hall, Durban, on the eve of the Indian day of protest against the Group Areas Bill.

R. P. Erasmus is the Vice-President of the South African Mineworkers' Union. In 1922 he led the greatest strike in the history of South Africa. Thirteen thousand strikers were organized as armed commandos. Johannesburg was under martial law. Over seven hundred people lost their lives. It was the upheaval that overthrew the Smuts government. Erasmus was the "Kommandant-Generaal," and in South Africa he is still known as General Erasmus. After the strike was quelled, Erasmus was captured and sentenced to death. His sentence was commuted to hard labor and after three years an embittered man took up the cause of the mineworkers again.

Erasmus came to *The Forgotten Factor* the same night as one of the managers of his mine. At the age of sixty-six he is still an underground miner. The following day the manager said to him, "Erasmus, last night I saw *The Forgotten Factor*, and never again will I treat any man as of less value than myself." Erasmus replied, "Never again will I advocate a strike when we can settle our differences this way."

For some months he quietly worked out his convictions, saying little outside. Then he was at a reception given by the mayor of the gold-mining town of Springs. After some formal speeches Erasmus rose and asked if he might say something. Everyone was interested, for his background was well known. He said, "After *The Forgotten Factor* I sat down to tea with a mine manager. It is my first time in forty years in the mines that it has happened. We are annihilating one another in the world. I once saw a fight between a baboon and a bulldog. At the end the baboon lay dead and the dog had to be destroyed. We have been like that, but now things are different. If teamwork becomes reality, light will rise again. Otherwise we go down into the darkness."

Erasmus is a Nationalist. He fought under Paul Kruger and still feels passionately the experiences of the Boer war. Tears poured down his cheeks when he visited the house on Lake Geneva where the old President died in exile. In 1949 Erasmus opposed the mineworkers taking part in Caux. In 1950 he advocated sending a delegation at the expense of the union. The president, vice-president, and organizing secretary all came.

They told how a dispute recently arose which was exactly similar to one which had earlier vexed the industry for two years. A conciliation board, representative of the government, the union and the employers' Chamber of Mines, was set up. "I had become sick and tired of the continual struggle in our industry, and thought the Chamber might now feel the same," said the miners' president. "So I proposed that an adjournment should be granted while the two sides considered the matter in the light of Moral Re-Armament. As a result, settlement was reached within a fortnight." A management observer commented, "This is a settlement without precedent in the industry's history."

The Organizing Secretary of the Union, Mr. E. R. van Rensburg, who visited Caux later than the others, restated his president's opinion that relations between the mineworkers and the Employers' Federation were now on the best of footings as a result of Moral Re-Armament.

"In addition to the normal problems between workers and management we face a color issue in South Africa," he said. "I shall do everything in my power to see that the color question is solved above party politics and through the guidance of God."

Erasmus was invited to England. "That is no place for me," was his first reaction. But finally he decided to come, and much kindness was shown to him. One of the people he met was Lord Hardinge of Penshurst, private secretary to three successive British kings. There were three reasons, said Erasmus, why he should dislike Lord Hardinge. First he was British, second he was "upper class," and third he was a "capitalist." But Moral Re-Armament gave them a true basis for trust and friendship.

As Erasmus flew back to South Africa a treasured possession was a picture of the two of them together. He said, "I will drop every bit of bitterness into the sea as I fly back." In Johannesburg he reported to a meeting on his trip, "I came to England and I met a lot of changed Englishmen and I learned a lot of things from them."

The Erasmus home has been remade. Most of the money Erasmus earned used to be spent outside the house. Now they have a new carpet and a sofa and chairs. His wife says, "I didn't always look forward to his return. Now I just cannot wait for the moment he comes in."

After his return to South Africa, Erasmus routed the advocates of class warfare who attacked him in the union, by demonstrating that the miners had won more ground on the basis of Moral Re-Armament in one year than by other methods after many years of struggle.

II

In terms of the future of Africa, few groups are more important than the colored students from that continent who come to Britain to complete their training. All of them hope to rise to positions of leadership on their return to Africa, and many of them have already won distinction and achieved much among their own people.

In Britain, however, they often meet difficulties. In the words of a successful young artist from the Gold Coast, "We are quickly disillusioned when we try to get lodgings. It's easy to obtain a list of addresses, but quite another matter to find a landlady willing to entertain a colored student. The result is that many of us have to live in crowded hostels, completely

cut off from English home life. Naturally enough, we tend to
stick to ourselves, and the resentment and bitterness we feel
turns inward. Most educated Africans come to Britain with
already strong nationalist feelings. These feelings grow as we
are excluded more and more from personal touches with English people."

The Communists take endless trouble over these African
students—future leaders in their nations. For example, they are
told that they can obtain *free* training at Charles University,
Prague, in almost any subject from zoology to atomic research.
A number of them have accepted this tempting offer, little
realizing its full implications.

Also Communist homes are wide-open to colored students
and they are made very welcome there. After a while they are
invited to Communist meetings and given the chance to speak
on color problems. Today the majority of colonial students
find themselves much in sympathy with Communist ideas. The
reasons for the success of Communism are summed up by one
of the Africans as follows:

(1) Communists treat us better than the non-Commu-
nists do.
(2) They promise—and in fact do practice—freedom from
the color bar.
(3) They promise freedom for the colonial people from
economic exploitation.
(4) They promise self-government immediately.
(5) They encourage and exploit the racial bitterness latent in any people who are ruled by another race.

Between 1947 and 1950 over seventy African students came
to Caux, and the majority of them left determined to bring
Moral Re-Armament to their countries. One such student,
after a brief visit to Caux in 1949, returned to his university
intent on bringing an answer to the bitterness that existed
among his fellow countrymen, some of whom had even inter-

rupted their work to study the use of explosives and the technique of revolution. Within six months, through his efforts
and with the help of some of the local residents, the whole
atmosphere among those students had begun to change. The
following year six of them came with him and his wife to
Caux.

Aaron Obonna is a medical student from Nigeria. At Caux
he heard people explaining in practical and simple terms how
the application of absolute moral standards and the guidance
of God had transformed their own lives and begun to affect
the life of their nations. On the day he left Caux he said, "At
first I felt within me that people wanted to entertain us with
literary experience. Now I know that what they say from this
platform is real. In my guidance this morning I wrote, 'By
propounding the ideology of MRA and passing it on to us in
Africa, Frank Buchman has righted the many wrongs of the
whites to the colored races. We shall accept and uphold this
ideology and shall bear it forever. This is the only hope for
Africa, nay, for all nations.'"

A British official, who has been a member of the colonial
administrative service for the last sixteen years, heard Aaron
Obonna speak at Caux. He said, "A great issue of the second
half of the twentieth century is what ideology will grip the
colored peoples of the world. If they turn to Communism it
will be because we have failed to offer them a bigger alternative. It has taken me a long time to realize this truth. Obonna
mentioned the wrongs done by the white races in Africa. I
have not readily accepted that. My family—my father and
grandfather on both sides—have served for generations in
Africa, India, and other places. We have been mighty proud
of the work we have done there. But if the colored peoples of
the world do not want the sort of 'democracy' we show them,
whose fault is that? There has been deep in my thinking an
attitude toward the African people which said, 'Look what
we are doing for you! Look at all our hard work.' I demanded
gratitude and was resentful when I didn't get it. I begin to see

the wrongs white people have done to colored people in many parts of the world and I am sorry for them. Our greatest need in Africa is an ideology to inspire men and to change men, and on which black and white can unite. That is precisely what the ideology of Moral Re-Armament is doing. I want to back these Africans wholeheartedly in their fight for a new Africa based on absolute moral standards and the guidance of God. To do that effectively I know that I must start with a fundamental change in my own attitude."

III

Dr. Nnamdi Azikiwe, known to millions of people as Zik, is President of the National Council of Nigeria and the Cameroons and one of the most powerful figures in West Africa today.

He is forty-six, a married man with four children. He is a member of the Ibo tribe and his father intended to send him to Britain for his education. But a British officer one day insulted his father, so he decided to send Zik to America instead. The boy showed courage and character there. He worked for his college fees as a coal-miner, a dishwasher, laborer, and even a boxer.

He graduated at Lincoln University and became Master of Science at the University of Pennsylvania. He also distinguished himself in athletics. At the British Empire Games of 1924, while training at the White City, London, Zik felt himself and his race insulted by some of the Commonwealth competitors. He dropped his English name "Benjamin" and has never used it since.

In 1935 he returned to West Africa and built up a chain of newspapers. There are now five of them, which are read by many thousands of Nigerians, and the extent of their influence exceeds that of any other newspaper group in Nigeria.

In 1946 Zik was elected President of the National Council for Nigeria and the Cameroons. This is a council of about two hundred trade unions, political parties, and tribal unions. Each year since then he has resigned and been re-elected.

In recent years there has been a strong feeling in Nigeria that the constitution should be revised and the Africans given more say in their own affairs. Zik, as President of the National Council, pressed for revision. The British authorities at first told him he "represented nobody."

Zik thereupon stood for the Legislative Council and was elected by a decisive majority. The British authorities still regarded him with great suspicion. So Zik toured for nine months, visiting every part of Nigeria, and returned with support from his people to go to England to see the Secretary of State with proposals for a fifteen-year plan toward dominion status. He had a bad reception in England. He was smeared by sections of the press, and the outcome of his visit was that he was told to "go home and co-operate."

On his return home his organization tore up their proposals for constitutional reform and produced the more radical "Freedom Charter," which demands self-government *now* outside the British Commonwealth. In October 1949, Zik embarked on the next stage of his campaign. Having failed to convince the Nigerian Government or the British Colonial Office with his original proposals, his organization decided to send delegates to any international body that would give them a platform.

Zik was invited to address the "Congress of Peoples against Imperialism," held in London, then to proceed to Prague for a conference on "Human Rights" and to visit Moscow.

On his arrival in England Zik was again attacked by sections of the British press. "Black Mischief" was one headline, above a full-length picture of Zik.

He was invited to spend an evening in a London home, where he was welcomed with simple warmth and treated as an honored guest by his English host. It was here that he learned about Moral Re-Armament. "In all the times I have been to London," he remarked, "this is the first time I have ever been treated as an equal in somebody's private home."

He and the Federal Secretary of his party were invited to Caux. They accepted. Zik later described what he found there as "an island of peace in a sea of discord." He became aware of abundant evidence that human nature could be changed. At the end of three days he was able to say with deep conviction, "It's not a question of whether Nigeria is right or Britain is right, but *what is right for Nigeria*. Our prayer for Nigeria is, 'Through God's guidance the people of Nigeria shall be redeemed from the servitude of hate and fear and suspicion. The fire of love shall not be extinguished from the face of Nigeria. The torch of absolute honesty, purity, love, and unselfishness shall flame anew and bring not only a new Nigeria but the dawn of a new world in the making.'"

Soon after his return to London he had news of the loss of twenty lives when police opened fire on strikers at the Enugu coal mines. At once pressure was put on him by African members of the Communist Party to give orders for retaliation, and also to bring out the railway workers on strike. Zik steadfastly refused. Instead he sent a cable which was said to have done much to calm the situation.

In the teeth of strong pressure he canceled his plans to visit Prague and Moscow. This was a costly decision for him. The London *Daily Worker* attacked him on account of it and it was hinted that things would be made difficult for him when he got home. He saw the Colonial Secretary before he left England, and *The Times* quoted him as saying he hoped there would be "good sense now and better understanding on both sides. He would be ready to modify his demands for complete independence if the British Government were prepared to change their attitude."

Zik flew back to Nigeria. Some of his principal political enemies were among those who greeted him at the airport.

He took one of them home in the car with him. On the way he said that he was sorry for the political rivalry that had existed between them and that in the interest of unity he wanted to serve under him and co-operate with him.

One of Zik's chief aims has been to unify the political parties of Nigeria. In this task he draws constantly on the lessons he learned at Caux. Like many other men, he is not yet a saint —but a new ideology has begun to change his approach to problems. In a major political speech recently he concluded by relating his experience of Caux and warning the audience of the tendency to point an accusing finger at the other man, forgetting that three other fingers would point backward at the accuser. "The element of change of attitude is the forgotten factor which should enter the political life of Nigeria," continued Zik. "The point should not be who of our opponents is wrong, but what is right. There is no reason why Nigeria should not have the spirit of Caux."

His papers began to publish news of Moral Re-Armament's fight for a new world order, including verbatim reports of Buchman's speeches. And in a cable to a friend Zik says:

"Since my return to Nigeria the Caux spirit has worked wonderfully in our local politics. You will be glad to learn that I have become reconciled with all my former political enemies. . . . Nigerians are happy but flabbergasted. They are wondering what brought this about. Yes, the forgotten factor is responsible, thanks to Frank Buchman. The spirit of Caux is miraculous."

Meanwhile, Zik and his party, whose policy had been to hold themselves aloof from the official discussions on the revision of the Nigerian constitution, have now taken an active part. Zik also played a leading part recently in settling a labor-management dispute involving thirty thousand workers by bringing together the two sides in an amicable settlement. In an editorial headed "The Spirit of Caux," his principal newspaper, *The West African Pilot*, stated on June 5, 1950:

"The questions on every lip are therefore these: Is the African capable of realizing his destiny? Is he capable of generating a sufficient amount of intellectual and moral influence to coun-

teract the forces of evil? We believe he can. But in that belief
we submit that both leadership and followship require the
spirit of Caux. . . . That is the only gateway to African freedom."

In the 1950 Lagos election, Zik's party swept the polls, winning eighteen out of twenty-four seats.

But toward the end of the year some of Zik's extremist followers tried to drive him along the path of violence. Zik could
not reconcile this course with absolute moral standards. He
announced that he would retire from politics.

The London *Daily Worker* at once attacked him on the
front page, declaring that "since visiting the Moral Re-Armament headquarters in Switzerland he has largely abandoned
his fight." At the same time a member of a recent government
commission to Nigeria reported, "The whole country is talking about the change in Zik."

Zik's announced retirement created so much concern among
the people that in 1951 he came back into the political arena.

He made a speech in Lagos in which he declared, "I am at
your service. If we are to realize self-government now, then
nationalist forces must forget their petty selves and work
together for the glory of Nigeria. There is a need for change
of heart on the nationalist part. Former political enemies should
rid themselves of their suspicions and distrust, resolve their
differences, and be reconciled to each other. By cultivating in
our lives absolute standards of purity, unselfishness, honesty,
and love we can integrate rather than disintegrate our forces.
Then we can establish a positive ideology and proceed to realize our dreams."

XII. CAUX

•

Once the world looked to democracy as the door to the future. But today the millions are skeptical. They see democracy on the defensive, while from every side they are assailed by the plausible logic and daring attack of militant materialism. It seems to them to offer the only open road.

Can democracy re-win her lost place in the hearts of the millions?

For the past five years at Caux there has been demonstrated a way of living democracy which has caught the imagination of men and women of every race, background, and culture. It has equipped them with a revolutionary zeal to make the ideology of inspired democracy the dominant factor in their nation's life.

Thirty thousand delegates from 103 countries have been to the assemblies at Caux. They include ten prime ministers and ninety-three cabinet ministers, as well as trade union officials from thirty-four countries, men who lead forty million workers.

Two thousand Marxists and Communists have come to find a superior ideology.

Fourteen United States Senators [26] and twenty-three members of the House of Representatives are among the delegations from the Parliaments of the world that have come to Caux.[27]

[26] See Document 26, "The Brightest Star," report by Senator Karl E. Mundt.

[27] See Document 27, "Caux," including report by official bi-partisan committee of the House of Representatives.

Twenty-one European nations, twenty-two of the African countries, twenty-two countries in the Americas, thirteen of the lands of the Moslem world and the Middle East have sent their delegations. Fourteen nations of the Far East have been represented. Caux is the Mecca of the right ideology.

In September 1950, when eighteen of India's leaders sought help in the ideological training of the nation, they applied not to Moscow, not to London, not to Washington—but to Caux.

The Foreign Minister of Denmark, speaking in February 1951 before a mass meeting at Copenhagen which included many of the leaders of the nation, said, "We are in the midst of a world struggle. . . . This (MRA) is a world movement which in its belief that it is possible to change the individual person and the individual nation is working above the boundaries raised up by creed, race, and different historical development. . . . This world movement will play its part in the shaping of the future. None of us can allow ourselves to remain indifferent. . . . The main thing is not to be cold or lukewarm, but to make up our minds."

Men are turning to Caux because it is providing for East and West, for all men everywhere, the secret of renaissance, the pattern of a world rebuilt.[27]

I

What is the magic of Caux that other conferences do not have?

The Vice-President of the French Senate said, "We have failed to unite Europe because we have tried to do it on a political and economic basis. We need the moral unity which we find at Caux." And a delegate to the United Nations stated, "In many conferences the problems round the table are greater than those on the table. Caux is the conference with a cure, for it deals with the factor that is not even on the agenda of other conferences—human nature."

[27] See section 3 of Document 27, "Reflections on the Secret of Caux," by the Catholic author, Count C. Lovera di Castiglione.

A leader of twenty-eight thousand airline workers in India came to Caux. In his heart there burned the memory of jailings and beatings. He arrived bitter, cynical, and hopeless. He began to change. When he faced the moral issues in his own life, he recognized the moral issues in the life of his nation. His philosophy had been that his country should be left to itself and stand aside while Russia and America fought it out between them and settled what the future of the world should be. Now he saw that it was not America or Russia, but men like himself in their millions who could shape the future. He left Caux determined to be a rebuilder of men. He returned as a constructive force to his own people, resolved to play his part with them in remaking the world.

He found deadlock in an aircraft plant that is one of the key spots in India's defense industry. He began by uniting the two warring factions inside the union. Then he tackled management effectively. He also made progress with the government department that concerned itself with that industry.

From all sides efforts were made to induce him to take a line that might be politically expedient but was wrong. He refused, even though he risked unpopularity by doing so.

The strike ended. All the men went back to work. Production has begun to rise.

The creation of new men is the normal and daily experience at Caux. It can become the normal practice of cabinets.

Caux deals with men and rebuilds them personally to the point where their approach to everything and everybody changes. Frank Buchman puts it this way: "It sounds in the nature of a discovery, but you need new people. An ideology which means new people, that is a superior ideology. It is a force that has to be reckoned with. The force of a superior idea. Isn't it a superior ideology if we have something better? Human nature changed and so utterly different that all men say of you, 'This fellow is a genius to live with.' It means new people at conferences—people who live differently, who act differently when they get home—radically different. This is the change labor expects from management and which will meet their demands more than halfway. With a chain of people living a superior ideology differences soon melt away and life becomes a joyous reality."

People find a life at Caux. Men of all faiths and men of no faith find absolute standards can be applied to their lives and to the lives of their nations.

A docker from Liverpool says, "No idea has ever come out of the Kremlin to equal the four standards of Moral Re-Armament."

Change is for everyone. It begins when these standards are applied drastically. Men with this experience have something real which they can pass on to others. And as men change they begin to enter a new dimension. For problems that seemed insoluble move swiftly toward an answer as the hates and greeds and fears of those who create the problems are dissolved.

At Caux men learn that human nature can be changed—but that only God can change it.

Faith becomes real to some, stronger to others, as this truth is tested by daily renewed experience. Thus a Moslem, if he lives up to the highest teaching of Islam and accepts absolute moral standards and the guidance of God, becomes part and parcel of the moral and spiritual awakening of his people, and so of the world. Without this living faith, he is as powerless as a nominal Christian.

Men, rebuilt and with a faith, articulate that faith in such a way that every problem affecting their nation and the world is brought within its compass. When the moral and spiritual causes of each deadlock are recognized, the answer comes in sight.

That is how at Caux Communists and capitalists, management and labor, men of every class and race, find the unanimity that the world is awaiting.

This does not mean that all who come to Caux feel the same way about every issue. They do not. But they do learn there the secret of how to rise above considerations of party, class, race, point of view, or personal advantage. At that level, unity is found.

II

Caux is also the pattern of the new society. It is a common life of people from all races and classes, who seek the guidance of God in their actions and policies. It foreshadows the life we might have in any situation where enough men unitedly determine to make the Will of God the will of the people. It brings the secrets of Divine Wisdom within the reach of the ordinary sinner and the ordinary skeptic. Thousands at Caux have experienced that when man listens, God speaks; when man obeys, God acts.

This forgotten truth has become the way to reunited homes, to effective economic planning, to new unity between men and nations. It was in a time of silence that Irène Laure, the Frenchwoman, found the answer to the bitterness that burned in her heart against Germany. A German leader says her visits to that country since she found that secret have done more to unite Germany and France than all the conferences of the years.

The dockers come to Caux. The 1949 dock strike in Britain is estimated to have cost that country £217 million. A man who played a leading part in that strike gives his view that the British docks might have been on strike again twice since then were it not for what he and some of his friends had learned at Caux. They had begun to find the superior wisdom that comes to those who are humble enough to realize that human wisdom is not the last word. "I listen to God," one of them says, "and write down my thoughts in this notebook. This notebook is more important to me than my briefcase, for in it in quiet I write down the answer to the problems I carry around in my case."

Who can compute the millions of money and taxes that will be saved to the nation when the conferences and committees that sit without ceasing in every continent and country debating the problems of the hour are conducted in the spirit of Caux?

Men of every background find in an experience of guidance the bridge over every division. The Nigerian delegates say it is the answer to the bitterness between the colored and white races. A man who had the responsibility of training one hundred thousand workers of an industrial area of Europe in the principles of Marxism sees management begin to apply the secret of guidance. He says, "When management begins to speak with the voice of Caux, the class struggle is out of date." He goes back to his country and gives the workers training in this ideology of the heart and conscience.

And Communists tear up their Party cards at Caux, for listening to the voice of guidance opens the door of faith for the schooled materialists. It starts as a practical experiment and becomes a proved experience.

The conception of a new world that Caux offers is so vast, yet so personally satisfying, that the Communist says he cannot resist it. He sees in this renaissance of society the answer to bloody revolution, because in the fire of renaissance the steely selfishness and iron injustice which have produced the philosophies of force will melt away.

Caux is beginning to reverse the historic process of infiltration which for so long has riddled the state departments, the trade unions, the schools of the democracies. Now the Communists are going back to their cells and their Party organizations with the force of an answering ideology which wins their comrades to a greater revolution. For they carry in their own experience the answer to the basic assumptions of the materialist faith.

Caux dares to seek the mind of God on the problems which the mind of man has created.

III

Caux also offers the world a trained ideological force and weapons for its use. Let Frank Buchman in his own words describe how such a force was built:

"A generation ago a group of men gripped by a materialist ideology decided to capture the world with it. They gave their lives to that task. For twenty-five years they have worked —every hour, sleeping and waking, ceaselessly, skillfully, ruthlessly on a world front.

"Suddenly the statesmen of the democratic nations have woken up. They rub their eyes as they see what is happening. Why, they ask, are we in this situation? How did it come about?

"The reason is simple. While many slept, and others busied themselves with their own affairs, the materialists have been working out their revolution with a philosophy, a passion, and a plan.

"What is the answer? A generation ago the force of Moral Re-Armament began fighting too. On a world front it has been answering plan with plan, idea with idea, a militant godless materialism with a militant inspired ideology for democracy.

"The idea caught hold. It remade men. It impacted nation after nation. Now it girdles the globe.

"Today at the Moral Re-Armament Assembly at Caux we see this force in action with the answer, available for service. At a time when statesmen realize the lateness of the hour, it freely offers the fruit of twenty-five years of toil."

In the words of Foreign Minister Schuman of France, it provides "teams of trained men, ready for the service of the state, apostles of reconciliation and builders of a new world."

And at a time when the democratic nations are searching for means to dramatize their cause to the world, Caux has created ideological weapons which have already proved highly effective in reaching the millions. *The Forgotten Factor* has been translated into twelve languages and has been seen by audiences totaling over 850,000, comprising the leadership of eighteen countries.[7] *The Good Road* [28] revue has dramatized the ideas of democracy for tens of thousands in Europe and America. Five other plays have had their equally vital part in reaching minds confused by subversive ideas.

Through its plays, revues, and songs Moral Re-Armament is sowing the seeds of a renaissance of the arts which promises to bring a new theater and a new culture to the world.

IV

At Caux a living formula is emerging which is the answer to Communism.

Communism succeeded in establishing a new thinking and bringing it within the reach and range of the ordinary man. It has enabled him to interpret every world event in terms of the class struggle.

That is why Communists, all over the world, act ideologically in each situation in which they find themselves. Whether he be a statesman at the United Nations, a trade unionist at a labor meeting, an ordinary man reading his newspaper, the Communist interprets events and bases his actions upon a common ideological conception. This ideological approach applies to every sphere—politics, industry, education, literature, art, even sport. Stalin puts it this way: "The strength of our ideology consists in the fact that it enables the Party to orient itself in any situation, to grasp the internal connection of events, to foresee the course of events, and to discern not only how and when events are developing now, but also how and when they must develop in future."

But Caux also is establishing a new thinking and bringing it within reach and range of the ordinary man. It is giving the

[7] See Document 7, *The Forgotten Factor*.
[28] See Document 28, "The Chance to Save Civilization" by Rear Admiral Richard E. Byrd.

world an ideology more universal and more fundamental than
that of Communism; an ideology that pervades every aspect
of life and enables all men to act ideologically and effectively
in every situation. It is, moreover, an ideology of choice, not
of coercion; an ideology of freedom, not of force.

It substitutes for the theory of the inevitable struggle between class and class, race and race, the fact of the everlasting
struggle between good and evil. It offers this struggle as the
background for each decision of the human heart and will.

Frank Buchman sums it up, "A faith moves Communists. A
greater faith will need to capture us to give us the power of
a supernational thinking to build the new world which is our
rightful heritage. This is the disciplined living we need. It is
not connivery that will run the new world. It is men God-led
who will change history, who will give us a nation God-led
that will remake the world.

"We must recapture the faith that has eluded us. Our
grandfathers and our grandmothers had it. Lincoln was a man
who had that faith. He knew God, and he united a nation. It
needs men whom God can talk to, to fashion and unite a new
world."

XIII. FRANK BUCHMAN

●

It is given to few men to be a full generation ahead of the time in which they live. Such men are centers of controversy to their contemporaries and a cause of thankfulness to succeeding generations. It has always been so in history. It is so with Frank Buchman.

Frank Buchman is an American of distinguished Swiss descent. One of his ancestors was the successor to Zwingli in Zurich and translator of the Koran into German. After his family came to America in 1740 they settled in Pennsylvania. One ancestor fought with Washington at Valley Forge. Another was the first man to enlist in Abraham Lincoln's army during the War Between the States.

Today Buchman is seventy-three years old. He is widely traveled and his knowledge of countries is profound, as it is drawn from a personal knowledge of people and leaders in all parts of the world. After leaving college he traveled extensively each year and, though he held university positions at the State College of Pennsylvania and elsewhere, he devoted as much time as possible to getting to know men and countries.

In the year 1921 he was invited by a British military adviser to join him at Washington during the Disarmament Conference. It was a significant occasion for two reasons. First, because on the train to Washington the impelling thought filled Buchman's mind, "Resign, resign, resign!" He faced the moral challenge to be willing to abandon the financial security and comfort of a salaried position for an unknown road. Second, because the conference sessions confirmed his conviction that plans for world peace were inadequate unless they reckoned with the necessity of a change in human nature. "You can plan a new world on paper," he often says, "but you must build it out of people."

Soon he was enlisting and training people of every stratum of society to bring to their nations a basic change in economic, social, national, and international relationships, all stemming from personal change. Within a few years, through the impact of a returning group of Rhodes Scholars who had met him in Oxford University, Buchman's work was to acquire nation-wide significance in South Africa. The press of that country first bestowed on his friends the title of "The Oxford Group."

It was to these developments that the Hon. J. H. Hofmeyr, for many years Smuts' Deputy Premier, referred when he said, "Buchman's visit to South Africa in 1929 was of national significance and started a major and continuing influence for racial reconciliation throughout the whole country, white and black, Dutch and British. . . . The future of democratic institutions in South Africa may well depend largely on the fruits of their labors."

The work spread rapidly. By the thirties it had become world-wide. Norway's delegate at Geneva, later to become President of the League of Nations, said, "Where we have failed in changing politics, you have succeeded in changing lives, and given men and women a new way of living."

In 1938, realistically facing the fact that armed conflict could not finally decide the ideological issue in the world, Buchman launched the program of Moral Re-Armament [33] which stated the need of moral force to win a war and to build a just peace. Of this program he says, "God gave me the thought, 'There will be a mighty movement of moral and spiritual re-armament that will reach the corners of the world. New men—new nations—a new world.' " [34]

[33] See Document 33, "Launching of Moral Re-Armament."
[34] See Document 34, "What Are You Living For?"

I

Frank Buchman's insight and action began to stir the nations to prepare for the ideological conflict. This was precisely what the Fascists and Communists feared most, that to the industrial and armed might of the democracies should be added the superforce of an inspired ideology. His action roused the best patriotic forces in the democracies and inevitably the opposition of the subversive forces. As early as 1917 his experiences in the Far East had taught him the godless basis of Communism. And Communists were quick to realize that the moral and spiritual renaissance which he brought was their most dangerous enemy. Likewise he clearly understood the basic materialism of Fascism.

In 1945 he stated a basic truth which had not yet wholly dawned on the statesmen of the West. "Today we see three ideologies battling for control. There is Fascism and Communism, and then there is that great other ideology which is the center of Christian democracy—Moral Re-Armament. We need to find an ideology that is big enough and complete enough to outmarch any of the other great ideologies. Until that time comes, men will flounder. They will not find their way."

From the beginning he was heavily attacked by all who did not wish to see a moral ideology take root in the world. The Communist attacks were based on the usual technique of calling anyone they feared a Fascist. The Nazis said that his work "supplies the Christian garment for world democratic aims. . . . The members are challenged to place their lives under the Cross of Christ as opposed to the swastika which seeks to destroy the Cross of Christ. It is clearly opposed to National Socialism."

Yet some of the very people who told Buchman "leave us alone" or "go and change Hitler," and whose own complacency almost sold out the democratic cause a few years after, were the people who later hinted that MRA's efforts in Germany proved that Buchman was pro-Nazi. The fact is that Buchman never met Hitler, and (Hitler was too cautious to get into Buchman's orbit.) Nor was Buchman an intimate of Himmler or of any other member of the Nazi hierarchy.

The influence of Buchman's work did stretch into Nazi Germany, just as today it is penetrating behind the Iron Curtain. Indeed, Ludendorff's magazine at one point warned solemnly that "the sweet poison of Moral Re-Armament is seeping over our borders." (Small wonder that, even before the war, the Nazis banned MRA literature.) Their invading armies had instructions to suppress MRA wherever they went.

Were these facts not in themselves a tribute to Buchman's effectiveness? And might not history have taken a different turning, if the democracies had themselves been armed with an ideology of change and known how to bring it to Germany and to every nation in the years between the wars?

Today when events have been successively proving the rightness of Buchman's ideological insight, while continuing to stress the danger of Communism he has increasingly emphasized that anti-Communism is not a cure. The answer, he says, lies in a moral and spiritual ideology adequate to cure the moral weaknesses in our civilization and creative enough to win the allegiance of masses of people in every land who justifiably look for change. "The only sure victory," he says, "lies in this compelling answer backed by the sure right arm of military strength, so that our statesmen may not be out-thought, and our armies out-fought."

II

Through the war years, Buchman fought ceaselessly for the creation of that ideological clarity and moral strength which he saw to be essential both for the winning of the war and in order to provide the basis of a lasting peace.

As early as June 1941, for example, six months before Pearl Harbor, he said in Philadelphia:

"The aim of Moral Re-Armament is a nation fortified against attack from within and without. It is a national necessity.

"Moral Re-Armament creates the qualities that make democracy function. It gives to every man the inner discipline he needs and the inner liberty he desires. It calls out and combines the moral and spiritual responsibility of individuals for their immediate sphere of action.

"It builds for democracy an unshakable framework of actively selfless and self-giving citizens, whose determination to bring unity cannot be altered by any beckoning of personal advantage and who knows how to pass along to others their panic-proof experience of the guidance of God.

"These men are true fighters—patriots who have been fighting daily over long periods to bring this needed boon to our nation. . . . They are out to break the bottleneck of confusion and division and to anticipate the strategy of the subversive forces."

It was at this time that Mr. Truman, then Chairman of the Senate Committee for the investigation of America's war effort, said that he "felt a fresh certainty about the safety and security of America because of the evidence everywhere I go of the spread of Moral Re-Armament."

At the war's end Buchman was in San Francisco when the conference met to draft the United Nations Charter. A group of delegates invited him to present the program of Moral Re-Armament through the medium of *The Forgotten Factor* to the members of the conference.[30] Coming in the middle of the protracted and at times dispiriting debates on the terms of the UN Charter, it stirred such enthusiasm that more performances had to be arranged. Invitations multiplied from delegates asking Buchman to bring trained task forces to assist in the reconstruction of their war-ravaged countries.

The world response to this ideology has led a British diplomat to evaluate Buchman's work in these words: "The first

[30] See Document 30, "At Work in San Francisco."

point is that he saw the significance of this underlying ideological struggle years ahead of most other public figures, and his published speeches over the past ten and fifteen years prove it.* But he did not stop there. He did a second thing. He faced the consequences of this ideological struggle and began to think out what democracy's answering positive ideology was. And then he did a third thing. He built a world force of people ideologically equipped and living out the answer in their own lives. And that is Moral Re-Armament."

The spirit in this world-wide force is reflected in the preamble to the Articles of Incorporation of Moral Re-Armament in the United States:

"Riches, reputation, or rest have been for none of us the motives of association.

"Our learning has been the truth as revealed by the Holy Spirit.

"Our security has been the riches of God in Christ Jesus.

"Our unity as a world-wide family has been in the leadership of the Holy Spirit and our love for one another.

"Our joy comes in our common battle for a change of heart to restore God to leadership.

"Our aim has been the establishment of God's Kingdom here on earth in the hearts and wills of men and women everywhere, the building of a hate-free, fear-free, greed-free world.

"Our reward has been in the fulfilment of God's Will."[31]

III

Although statesmen have sought his aid, sometimes publicly and more often privately, although he is, humanly speaking, the leader of a major world force, yet Buchman has never lost his humor, and his unique caring for individuals and their needs has grown through the years.

In this task of remaking the world to which he has dedi-

* *Remaking The World.*
[31] From *The Oxford Group* by J. P. Thornton-Duesbery. See Document 31, "Challenge to the Contemporary World."

cated himself he has shown another great quality rare in our
time, of developing and training others to take responsibility.
He often says, "You have never succeeded unless you have
trained ten men to do your work better than you can do it
yourself." The continuance of his life work is secured for the
future by the principle of revolutionary teamwork. Through
it, cells and national teams have already been built in all countries of the world to which there is free access of a moral and
spiritual ideology, and even behind the Iron Curtain.

His love for people, his sensitiveness to their needs and fail-
ures, his gift for creating in them the will to live their best, is
an art. It is the secret of the growth of his work. It is an art
which he says can be normal for every man. A Scottish miner,
Peter O'Connor, said of an interview which he had with
Frank Buchman, "In my half hour with you I was helped
more than by any other living soul." To which Buchman
commented, "It is not my art. It is God's art."

To receive guidance from God is for him as normal an experience as eating or sleeping. He often remarks that "God
gave a man two ears and one mouth. He ought to listen twice
as much as he talks."

"Just as television is that space-conquering vision on the
material plane," he once said in a world broadcast, "so guidance is the far-seeing perception on the spiritual. It is limited
only by our capacity for disciplined obedience.

"Guidance is when we are in communication with God.
The first step in re-orienting our minds to God is to listen
twice as much as we talk. This is a simple program of how to
begin. Yet here lies the strategy to win the world from her
egocentric ways. For immediately self is the center of the
picture, there war has begun, whether in individuals or in nations. Fear is another kind of guidance. People are afraid, and
so they will not fight the daily battle against selfishness.

"Guidance is an absolute necessity and the irreducible
minimum to keep millions spiritually and physically alive. It
is the nation's lifeblood. Without it nations perish. Statesmen

living this quality of life will make it possible for the Mind of God to become the mind of nations. Through lack of this quality in their statesmanship, nations sell their birthright. 'If we are not governed by God, we will be ruled by tyrants,' said William Penn."

IV

Since engaging on this work thirty years ago Buchman has never had a permanent home. His force of fully trained personnel is in the hundreds. They work without salary, yet they never go hungry. Together with hundreds of thousands of men and women, ranging from housewives to cabinet ministers, they live out the truth that there is enough for everybody's need, but not for everybody's greed, and that when we care enough and share enough everybody has enough. Says Frank Buchman of this fact, "Where God guides, He provides."

Thousands of people convinced of the basic necessity of this answer sacrifice to advance this revolutionary force. There have rarely been large gifts. There have been thousands of small gifts, not from surplus, but from sacrifice. His work is financed and maintained in the spirit of the American Declaration of Independence: "With a firm reliance on the protection of Divine Providence we mutually pledge to each other our lives, our fortunes, and our sacred honor." From the early days Frank Buchman's work has advanced through the sacrifices of those who believe in it. Men offer for the faith they hold most dear the things they count most precious. People have given of their wages, their capital, their houses, their savings.

In Britain, for example, dockers, miners, and shop stewards in many parts of the country have formed "fighting funds." Workers may if they choose contribute to them. This enables their delegations to come to Caux and contribute to the running of the Assembly there.

A former European Communist, asked whether industrialists contributed to the funds of Moral Re-Armament, replied, "Some do. I wish more did. Every worker should rejoice when businessmen begin to invest in a force that is fighting effectively for social justice and a new world order."

The spirit of sacrifice among those at the heart of the work who, like Buchman himself, have given everything in the battle for a rebuilt world, wins a response from those who hear the message of MRA.

Those who have seen a new spirit transforming their homes, their industries, and their communities wish to do all they can to make this essential commodity available to others. People spontaneously make gifts from what they have—hospitality, time, talents, food, and other gifts in kind as well as money. At Caux, for example, such gifts were received as coal from the Ruhr, eggs and butter from Denmark, cutlery from Sheffield, and coffee from Kenya.

Some give to the work as and when they can. Others covenant to give regular sums for a specific period of years. There are also sales of MRA literature, and sums from these sales are available for the general purpose of the work.

It is fair to say that the traditional economic theories of "enlightened self-interest" have landed the world in a mess. Frank Buchman is demonstrating on a world front the practical effectiveness of the economics of unselfishness.

Every dollar in MRA goes far further than in any business concern or government department. The advance of the work has been out of all proportion to the size of its budget. For when workers, however highly qualified or experienced, give service without salary, administrative costs are cut to a fraction. Hotels, garages, printing, medical and dental care are often provided free or at a minimum cost by those in every nation who wish to spread this ideology around the world.

Large numbers of people, themselves in regular work but

who may have little money to contribute, give up week-ends and evenings to undertake many necessary services.

Every activity of MRA is planned to combine the greatest advance of the work with the most economic use of funds and services so sacrificially provided.

v

Frank Buchman is a man with a host of friends across the world. His services to the Greek nation were recently acknowledged by King Paul who made him a Commander of the Royal Order of King George I of Greece. What he esteems most in life, however, is the friendship of innumerable men and women, whether former Communists or military and industrial leaders.

Typical is this letter received from a changed veteran Communist leader in the Ruhr, twenty-five years a member of the Party until he met Frank Buchman:

"The fight is tough but it is a fine thing and I am grateful to be able to be in it with my family. The Good must conquer. All my spare time I spend in talking with people about this ideology and also, as well as I can, I try to live as an example of it. I have many human mistakes and weaknesses to overcome, and my family also. God has to help us time and time again. But of one thing I am certain, I have never been so happy and so contented as I am today. That I owe to you.

"Now I must stop this pen-work and give you warmest greetings from all my family which consists of myself, my wife, my daughter, and my son-in-law. At the same time I wish you the best of health.

"But, above all, I wish success to this wonderful ideology in all lands, so that mankind can once again become happy."

XIV. THE WORLD REBUILT

•

Has democracy the strength to win?

History depends upon the reply to that question.

If democracy is to win, an answer must be found to subversive activity in docks and state departments, to industrial deadlock in the mines and mills, to corruption between citizens and officials, to division in the home.

All these things spring from a breakdown in human behavior. They are caused because millions of people have a deadened sense, in their private and public life, of what is *Right* and of what is *Wrong*.

Lenin understood the primacy of the moral cause in human affairs. He said that Communism and the class struggle can never succeed "until the myth of God is removed from the mind of man." He gave to the Communists this advice: "Postpone operations until the moral disintegration of the enemy makes the delivery of the mortal blow both possible and easy."

Abraham Lincoln put it this way: "At what point then is the approach of danger to be expected? I answer, if it ever reach us it must spring up among us; it cannot come from abroad. If destruction be our lot, we must ourselves be its author and finisher. As a nation of free men we must live through all time or die by suicide."

The theory of democracy offers the finest form of society known to man. But democracy is on trial today, not for its theory, but for its practice. The true voice of America is not a radio program, but the way each American behaves all the time, whether as a citizen at home or a soldier overseas.

(Moral Re-Armament is restoring absolute standards of Right and Wrong to the heart of individuals and the heart of nations.) It is building inspired democracy—a democracy that will win the world.

Where else is there a world force with a world strategy to out-revolutionize Communism and so to change it?

The moral re-armament of men and nations is a factor in world affairs today. Industrial deadlock *is* being resolved. Marxists *are* finding a new thinking. France and Germany *are* reaching a new level of unity. The peoples of East and West *are* discovering that the common bond of all men everywhere is their need for change. Homes *are* being rebuilt. A new honesty *is* being born between husband and wife, daughter and mother, father and son. Workers and employers in the docks and steel mills, the mines and factories *are* creating a new pattern for the wealth and labor of mankind. Youth *is* being captured by a creative enthusiasm. Military leaders *are* finding the secret of total preparedness.

Through Moral Re-Armament men and women, learning to re-establish true standards of Right and Wrong, to live them and to fight for them, are becoming effective in their communities and nations. One worker put it this way: "Where I work is not the whole world. But it's the world I live in. MRA works in my world. And if it works there it will work everywhere."

It need not this time be either world dictatorship or world war. It can be a world rebuilt—with everyone playing his part in the rebuilding.

The World Rebuilt begins in our own heart and home, and then is carried across the nation. Frank Buchman sums it up in these words:

"Human nature can be changed. That is the root of the answer. National economies can be changed. That is the fruit of the answer. World history can be changed. That is the destiny of our age."

... the ... Re-Armament ... restoration ... standards of living ... and power to the heart of production, and the heart of production is building up clear consciences. A democracy that works in the world.

Where one is where a world free, with a world strategy to win to humanize Communism and so to change it.

The moral re-armament of men and nations is a force as world affairs today. In favour of ... Before world.

Marxists are facing a new challenge, higher and stronger, as offering a new level of unity. The promise of Marx and Lenin ... the ...

... though Marx the Communist everybody seemed far than to re-establish the standard of life ... and Works, in the ... to fight for them, are becoming ... everywhere men and women are awakening to a creative enthusiasm. Marxist leaders are the first to speak of total revolution.

Human nature can be changed. That is the root of the answer. National economies can be changed. That is the trunk of the answer. World history can be changed. That is the destiny of our age.

PART TWO

•

Documents

1. MELTING THE IRON CURTAIN

•

In April 1951, an MRA international force visited
Miami by invitation of Eastern, Pan-American, and
National air lines, and leading industries and civic
authorities of the area. The following address of
welcome was broadcast from Station WIOD, Miami,
by Representative William H. Lantaff of South Florida, on Easter Day, March 25:

This is your Congressman—
Bill Lantaff—with my report to you from Washington.

For the past few weeks, the newspapers have been filled
with sordid stories about certain activities in connection with
obtaining RFC loans. The Senate of the United States is now
engaged in a great debate on the question of sending American troops to Europe. We all know from our own experiences about the high cost of living and increasing taxes. We
are experiencing the headaches and heartaches of a national
emergency, and our country is facing one of the most peril-
ous times in its history. When the House of Representatives
reconvenes after Easter, we will take up for debate a new
draft law and universal military training. Sensational stories
reach us every day of the influence wielded by criminal elements in high political circles.

These are surely troubled times, and, as your Congressman,
I feel a great sense of responsibility. I cannot help but wonder
if, in addition to the congressional investigations being conducted, we do not need to make an investigation of ourselves,
to determine whether or not we have not neglected our own

faith—faith in ourselves, faith in our country, faith in God. We in America fail to realize that the principles of democracy, when coupled with the principles of Moral Re-Armament, can be formed into an ideology much stronger than Communism. It is an ideology that can win the world.

For the next few minutes I would like to tell you of an unusual opportunity and privilege that we in south Florida have in store for us this coming week. In January, of this year, a National Assembly for Moral Re-Armament was held in Washington. Some fifteen hundred delegates from twenty-five countries attended this Assembly. Most of these people were from the United States and a number of prominent south Florida citizens were included in this group.

My wife and I attended a number of the Assembly sessions and witnessed two of their plays. (I can truthfully say that I have never been given so much hope that practical solutions could be found to the many problems which our country faces today. I saw a program that not only could produce national unity—but one that has world implications and gives the most realistic promise yet on the horizon for winning the hearts and minds of those who have been deluded by the false temptations of world Communism.

Among the most effective weapons in the arsenal of Moral Re-Armament are a number of dramatic stage productions which were presented in Washington. Two plays which were presented in Washington will be presented in Miami. One of them, *Jotham Valley*, is a musical based on a true story from the ranching country of the West. The other is an industrial drama—*The Forgotten Factor*—a realistic and forceful story of the needless strife between management and labor.

These plays will begin on Thursday night, March 29, at the Dade County Auditorium. Dates and certain times can be obtained from our Miami newspapers. As a means of impressing you with the professional quality of these plays, it might be well to say that because of the enthusiastic response accorded *Jotham Valley* in Washington, where members of

Congress and other government officials saw it, New York producers became interested and brought it to Broadway. Skeptical Broadway critics, seasoned veterans of the theater, delegates from the United Nations, and thousands of theatergoers agreed that here was not only a new breath of fresh air for the stage, but a breath of hope for America and the free world.

The investigations of gambling syndicates, and other aspects of organized crime, have put south Florida in the national news in somewhat of an unfavorable light. Perhaps some of these charges have been unfair but they most certainly indicate that there was a need for cleaning up in our own backyard. I sincerely believe that these plays and the visit of the Moral Re-Armament task force to south Florida give us an opportunity to rally behind an idea that will help this whole area to become strong, clean, and united. We in south Florida can take the lead in giving America a rebirth of the American spirit and the American dream—based on the simplest principles found on our coins "E Pluribus Unum" and "In God We Trust"—or in other words, teamwork under Divine Guidance.

On this Easter Day, many of us have already attended church and many awakened early for the sunrise services, but we all are thinking of the miracle which happened two thousand years ago and to which we pay homage today. In these times we live in an age of miracles—miracles of production—miracles of scientific discovery—miracles even in the power of destruction, and miracles in conquering space and time. Perhaps on this Easter Day, it is not too much to pray for a miracle of the spirit which will ease our tensions and bring the miracle of peace which all mankind longs for. Perhaps it may not even be too much to hope that the power that rolled away the stone on the first Easter Day might melt the Iron Curtain and unite the East and the West on a basis of common honesty and trust in Divine Guidance.

2. JOTHAM VALLEY

•

This comment by George E. Sokolsky on the play,
Jotham Valley, appeared originally in the *New York
Journal-American*, February 18, 1951.

We were discussing plays and
the question naturally arose as to what plays could young-
sters of 10 and 14 be taken. Not being converted speakeasy
sophisticates, we were weary of discovering that the play-
wright suffered the tortures of the damned seeking for a curtain line and finally came up with the novelty of a foul word,
spoken by an apparently innocent ingenue. That always gets
a laugh!

Also we wanted the children to feel that because they went
to the theater, they were not being influenced to believe that
sex is all there is to American life; that life has some finer aspects, some very decent moments, a moral side, if you please.

So we went to see *Jotham Valley*, a play put on with all
the skill of professional showmanship by a group who call
themselves moral re-armament. This is a musical, with songs
occasionally comparable to *Oklahoma!* and with a story that
is so real that it does happen in every home. A very good time
was had by all.

The essence of *Jotham Valley* is the melodrama of two
quarreling brothers, whose hatred brings misery to all their
neighbors, particularly when one brother deprives the valley
of water, because he, legally but not morally, controls the
water rights. Here is a struggle that is universal, for legal
rights do not suffice in a world that requires constructive living. Law passed by legislators is often not only inadequate
but, being the product of man, unsound. We have to live by

the laws of man, but natural law, the law of God, transcends the laws of man.

So in the end, in this play, the key of truth opens the hardened heart of the brother and he permits the water to gush forth, so that the cattle drink of God's bounty, and life is good. Also the brothers make up.

This plot is as simple as *Romeo and Juliet*, which is the simplest and most usual of stories, being nothing more than that boy loves girl, but the parents say no. Most really important plots are simple, just as great symphonies are written around little tunes. (To wit: Those notes in Beethoven's Fifth, which Winston Churchill turned into a V for victory.)

Simplicity, of itself, may not only be truth but interesting and even exciting. What is more simple than a single tree, growing out of a rock along a granite seashore, standing proudly in a gale. All the smudge that a modernist can hurl at canvas cannot equal the majesty of that one object against a barren sky. And yet, as the poet said, only God can make a tree.

So in *Jotham Valley*, it is the simplicity of plot, in a musical and engaging setting, which opens the mind to the truth that man can and does change his nature through the humility of faith.

It is not surprising that this play has encountered the opposition of the Communists and the homosexuals in the theater, the former because they do not want men to think that the nature of man can be elevated by his own will, and the homosexuals because they excuse their indecencies on the ground that they cannot help themselves. They say that they are not evil but just that way because they are just that way.

Jotham Valley is a good play for adults, but it is important that children and youth should see it. With grace and ease, it projects the idea that life can be made worth living once the human wants to live a worth-while life.

This idea is not novel, but it needs to be constantly reiterated. Men live by hate because they like to hate. When they cease to like to hate, they will cease to hate. The causes for hatred are often so trivial, so unimportant, as to be ridiculous when analyzed. I know of groups of men who hate each other with violence. Knowing both sides, I also know that these hatreds are the products not of conviction but of suspicion and habit. Reconciliation is difficult because who is the first to say: "I have been wrong and a fool," when both have been wrong and both are fools?

So goes the world and in the end comes war and death. If children and young people could see *Jotham Valley*, maybe they, too, might find the key to better living.

3. THE RISE OF A NEW SPIRIT

•

Delegates to the 1948 World Assembly at Riverside, California, marking the Tenth Anniversary of Moral Re-Armament were invited to the United States by a Committee of eighty-three Senators and Representatives of both parties. They were welcomed to Washington by the then Speaker of the House, Hon. Joseph W. Martin, by the President pro-tempore of the Senate, Hon. Arthur H. Vandenberg, and by the Assistant to the President and Mrs. John R. Steelman. Prior to the Assembly an address of welcome was made on the floor of the House of Representatives by Hon. John W. McCormack, then Minority Whip and now Majority Leader of the House. Extracts from this address follow:

Mr. Speaker, at Riverside, California, starting on June 7 and ending on June 14, is being held the World Assembly of the Moral Re-Armament Association, with distinguished delegates and representatives from twenty-four countries.

The meeting of the world assembly dedicated to the great work of moral re-armament, or a return to God by individuals and nations, is a matter of world-wide importance. Communicants and members of all creeds, they are uniting in a determined effort to get the world back on a sound pathway, which might well be termed "The Road to God."

Moral Re-Armament of all persons and all nations is the primary and real answer to the materialistic feelings and conditions so prevalent in the world of today. This period of materialism in my opinion will be followed by a long period of mutual faith on the part of the people of the world. History shows relapses from time to time but always followed by a recovery of spiritual truths and as a result the progress of mankind.

I congratulate those persons attending this world assembly. This work is not and will not be in vain. Moral Re-Armament is the pathway to world stability, world happiness, and world peace.

On November 3, 1939, our late lamented Speaker, Hon. William B. Bankhead, in connection with the meeting at that time, held on December 1, 2, and 3, of 1939, of the world assembly of this association, made a beautiful and effective radio speech, prophetic in its nature, which is most appropriate to refer to on this occasion and which I include in my remarks.

The Rise of a New Spirit

Extracts from an address by the Hon. William B. Bankhead, Speaker of the House of Representatives of the United States of America, over the National Broadcasting Company Blue Network, November 30, 1939.

Here in America, one effect of this rising tide of Moral Re-Armament has been a renewed hope for industrial peace in those communities where it has formed a common meeting ground between capital and labor, and between opposing factions within the ranks of labor.

As for party politics, I myself have observed its effect in

the Nation's Capital where in these troublous times we are only too apt to think of ourselves as Democrats or Republicans, rather than as first of all Americans. Never in my long experience in Washington have I found anything on which all parties in both Senate and House have so thoroughly agreed as on America's need, and our own need, for this new spirit. It is making many of us realize that if we sincerely want national unity it is no use expecting the other party to make all the first moves; that our own party has possible faults which need correction in the national interest; and that it is a patriotic duty to have a spirit of national cooperation here at home . . .

Certainly if any nation needs to learn how to work together, it is our nation. No special social or political insight is required to point out that in national unity alone lies national strength.

Turning to the world situation. Where we failed in our dreams for the original League of Nations, was in not allowing for the fact that no international system, however nobly conceived, can endure without a new spirit in the nations which compose it. "Peace," Dr. Frank Buchman stated in a recent broadcast, "is not just an idea. It is people becoming different." Those words are worthy of serious consideration. They both point out the folly of the past, and chart a course for the peacemakers of the future.

After all, nations, like men, are much alike—responding to the same promptings of self-interest, nursing the same hates, haunted by the same fears. Each is jealous of her place in the sun—anxious to enlarge this place if feasible, to maintain it if possible, to relinquish it only if necessary. Most nations will accomplish these ends by fair means if they can; by other means if they must.

The essential condition of peace is a new spirit between nations. Without this new spirit no general settlement will be possible. A well-known columnist wrote recently that every nation is guilty, in that every nation has sinned. A frank recognition that all are responsible for the present situation, would go far toward bringing peace to Europe. Peace based on such a spirit could make both sides winners in this war. Otherwise the only winners are likely to be those forces of destruction, relentlessly at work in every land, for which a world conflict is the historic hour of opportunity.

We stand today at a decisive moment in history. Forces of unmeasured strength are on the march. Is there a force which can rally the recuperative powers of mankind and win the race with chaos?

There is a force which can out-march all others and which, if we will, can shape the future. It is the mighty onslaught of a new spirit challenging men and nations to a change of heart. It is the cumulative effect of millions of people who listen to God and obey. Where we have been true to this spirit, man has prospered; where we have neglected it, nations have declined. Now is our chance to re-create for ourselves and for our children the way of true patriotism—the way of moral and spiritual force.

Our country must look to her defenses. But no material defenses can serve us long unless behind them there stands a united people, strong in spirit, conscious of a common mission, prepared for any sacrifice . . .

A nation's first line of defense is the character of her citizens and the inspiration of her leaders. A country rich in land, in trade, in tradition, but poor in faith, declines. A country rich in faith is rich in everything. Restore character to a nation and you restore strength. Restore faith and you restore greatness. For character is wealth and faith is power.

The forces which cause war are not confined to the Old World. Working here in America are the same materialism, the same clash of interests, the same blindness to real issues, the same lust to acquire or hold power. The "haves" want to keep, and the "have-nots" want to get. The way of sanity both in domestic and foreign policy is not to point the finger at the other party or the other nation. It is to start to remedy the world's ills where they most closely concern us—here in America . . .

If western civilization is to be preserved . . . Moral Re-Armament must become the mainspring of our national life and the touchstone of policy both at home and abroad.

All of us, whatever our race or creed, can apply this new spirit beginning with ourselves, our family, our business, our community. There must be an end to selfishness and ease. Every citizen must be mobilized to bring about that moral and spiritual preparedness which will enable America to stand secure.

If we can demonstrate that at last on this continent we have found the secret of unity and peace among men, then we can become the peacemakers of mankind—makers of the just peace that will be permanent. So prepared, we can decide aright the fateful issues of this hour. So prepared, America can face the future with confidence, and the world can face it with hope.

> Mr. Paul Hoffman, Administrator of the Economic Cooperation Administration, sent the following message to the Riverside Assembly:

You have our unlimited confidence and support. You are giving to the world the ideological counterpart of the Marshall Plan.

4. INSPIRED MORAL LEADERSHIP

●

> A cable sent to leaders in Europe, Asia, and Africa by the Chairmen and Members of the Senate Foreign Relations Committee and the House of Representatives Foreign Affairs Committee, May 2, 1951.

As members of Foreign Relations and Foreign Affairs Committees of the United States Senate and House of Representatives, we wish to add our support to the invitation extended you to attend the World Assembly for the Moral Re-Armament of the Nations at Mackinac Island, Michigan, June 1-12, and to the welcome already issued by our Michigan colleagues in Congress. Your presence in the United States, together with other distinguished leaders from Europe and Asia, can do much to focus the attention of the American people at this time on the positive steps that can be taken everywhere to answer the ideological threat of world Communism. We need such a demonstration of united strength in the field of inspired moral leadership without which our common military, political and economic efforts to save the free world will certainly be less effective. We are impressed with the practical evidence of what such active moral leadership has accomplished to establish democracy as a working force in danger areas that affect the future of your country and ours. We recognise the opportunity this Assembly offers to proclaim to the world an inspired experience of democracy based on moral standards and the guidance of God which is the greatest bulwark of freedom. We look forward to welcoming you on the occasion of your visit.

> SENATOR TOM CONNALLY, Chairman,
>   Foreign Relations Committee
> SENATOR ALEXANDER WILEY
> REPRESENTATIVE JOHN KEE, Chairman,
>   Foreign Affairs Committee
> REPRESENTATIVE JAMES P. RICHARDS,
>   Deputy Chairman
> REPRESENTATIVE CHARLES A. EATON

Representative Joseph W. Martin, Minority Leader in the House of Representatives and Former Speaker, sent the following telegram to Frank Buchman on June 8, 1951.

For the past twelve years I have kept close touch with your great work. Its effect on the world situation has been profound and it is doing more to bring the nations together than any other force I know. On behalf of my colleagues in Congress I extend congratulations and best wishes to you and the notable gathering of leaders of the free world now in session at Mackinac.

JOSEPH W. MARTIN, JR.

> Mr. William Green, President of the American Federation of Labor, wrote the following letter to labor leaders in Europe and Asia:

The chairmen and ranking members of the Foreign Relations and Foreign Affairs Committees of the United States Congress, and the Michigan Congressional delegation have joined in welcoming national leaders from abroad to the World Assembly for Moral Re-Armament, at Mackinac Island, Michigan, June 1-12, 1951. The American labor movement warmly supports this welcome and expresses the hope that you and others of our trade-union brothers from Europe, Asia, Africa, Australasia, and the Americas will attend this gathering and so contribute to the new world of liberty and justice we all desire.

WILLIAM GREEN

5. TURN ON THE LIGHT

•

> An address by Dr. Frank N. D. Buchman delivered at the opening session of the World Assembly for the Moral Re-Armament of the Nations at Mackinac Island, Michigan, June 2, 1951.

There is chaos and confusion in the world today. There are wars and rumors of wars. There is a strong militant force that is out to win the world. You encounter it everywhere—in the mines, in the docks, in far-away Korea, in Malaya, in Indonesia, in Australia. It is a global conflict. And people are really worried. Fear grips them. They haven't an answer.

What can a man say and do in thirteen short minutes? That is my job, to try and give you the answer.

All people, I know, want to live happily together. We don't want to be disturbed. But we have to be. It is a thing that affects our taxes, and things that affect our taxes touch everybody. And when they go high enough, we try to work out something, rightly or wrongly we try to find an answer.

Everywhere people are dissatisfied. In Milan I saw signs on buildings "Long Live Communism." What is the other sign to put up? "Long Live—what?" People aren't much united yet on the answer.

Party lines don't hold the way they used to. Democrats and Republicans, it doesn't seem to make much difference. Some are good and some—not so good. But what is so hard to find is the leadership, the type of man to be in Washington, the universal type of man that really meets people's deepest needs. There are so few in whom the people place their full confidence. It used to be a fairly easy job to be in Washington, wrought with honor. But now with the divergent views it is beginning to be a considerable nuisance. Unless a man has the art of giving something everybody wants. Today we need men who take God into their consideration and make Him dominant without piosity. Men who forgive their enemies. Men who can clearly decide.

In Britain it is some of the dockers who are giving this leadership. They used to be a problem. They caused strikes and turmoil. But they changed and they are the ones who sent to all the Members of Parliament, not only the Commons, but the Lords, a book about Moral Re-Armament which seems to them to have the answer. They sent it not only to the Labor Members, but to the Conservatives, and a man high in that Party acknowledges with eagerness that these dockers have what he hasn't had. Other people were not aware that he didn't have it. They thought it was enough that he was a Conservative, but he said, "You have shown me that class is wrong and that no class or person of any class is always right."

This is such a difficult lesson to learn, each thinking the other fellow better than himself. People are so filled up with their own importance that there isn't room for much more. We need a new altitude of living, something above what we have seen as yet. It is acknowledging the right and yielding the wrong. And it brings illumination.

We have lived in darkness so long. Thomas Edison once said to me in a conversation which lasted way into the hours of the morning, "Is Heaven lighted up?" I told him, "Of course. You don't have to bother about that. It's been lighted up long since. You did your job in lighting up the earth." Everything can have light. Why shouldn't politics have light? Then our disputes would have more light and less heat.

Turn on the light. More light. That is the answer to confusion. There is no reason for not seeing clearly.

We have all the modern means of having more light. We have electric light which Edison first gave to the world by lighting up one house. We have radar which penetrates fog. We have X-ray which enables us to look inside. But we are not using all God has given us. With all this light the world seems to be marching in vast columns to darkness.

Our faith must be illumined, must have light. So different faiths, all faiths, need this supernatural gleam. "Lighten with celestial fire." "God is my Light and my Salvation; whom shall I fear?" And this light needs absolute moral standards to spotlight where we and our nations need to change. These are the additions to our Christian practice that need furbishing and burnishing. These need to be activated. Lived by every man, they are the secret of success.

Here in the State of Michigan the laboratory of Thomas Edison has been given a permanent home in Greenfield Village by that other great American, Henry Ford. Why are the names Ford and Edison such a galvanizing force in modern life? They were far-seers. Is that the element we lack in modern-day statesmanship?

Henry Ford sent me this message, "Moral Re-Armament gives me hope for the future of our country and the world, because of the results that are being achieved."

Mrs. Edison, too, understood Moral Re-Armament. She said, "This light, like my husband's, must go into every home." And the son, Charles Edison, as Secretary of the Navy said, "Now more than ever I am convinced Moral Re-Armament shares equally in importance with material re-armament."

These men were pioneers of the new industrial age. That is why they understood Moral Re-Armament, this new spirit alight in the world.

World circumstances now may compel us each to strike a flint, and each one will have to get it for himself. And that is our hope.

Take the Ford plant at Dagenham in London. The Superintendent in charge of the Assembly Building says, "In the unsettled state of affairs after World War II, I tried the tough way with the men. One day the shop-stewards asked me if I would meet them to discuss our problems on the basis of the four absolute standards of Moral Re-Armament. These meetings have had nothing but the best results. We are getting production without having to drive men. The Building is running more economically today than ever before. Our efficiency was 99.43 per cent in April this year—better than anything we have had since the war."

This World Assembly gives witness to the fact that an illumination is spreading to the whole world. We are practical people. If a new gadget is to be put into the house, we will put it in. It may be television. Why not this far-seeing vision, this new illumination in every home?

What is it that makes Members of the Senate and House support this work? What is it that makes members of the Foreign Affairs and Foreign Relations Committees cable to the capitals of the world? There is a whole new level of statesmanship wrapped up in this. It is a statesmanship that turns our foes into friends. When Communism comes in, darkness follows just as night follows day. But a Cabinet Minister who had seen this happen in his country said, "If Communism is darkness at noon, Moral Re-Armament is sunshine at midnight."

That is why a founder and anchor man of the Communist Party of Norway, thirty-four years a Communist, is sitting in our midst today. Labor leaders, formerly Communist, from the Ruhr, from the London docks, from France and Italy, leaders in management from Europe and Asia, people of every creed and no creed, of every race and background find here the essence of truth, something they all accept, and say, "This is better than anything I have known before. It works." The industrialist says, "This is the thing the worker wants," and it is something, too, he finds he wants for himself, and enjoys.

Men who have been constantly wrestling with problems see where they themselves have been wrong. The problems and strife melt away. There is nothing left for them to do. One CIO leader said, "Now I can go to bed and have a good night's sleep. The problem is solved."

Men are here today who through change have become exponents of the new order. They have seen this revolution on the march. A year ago I was invited by the German Chancellor, Dr. Konrad Adenauer, to lead a meeting in the Ruhr to offset the Berlin Communist demonstration. One of the German newspapers came out next morning with the headline, "Berlin a Wash-Out. Moral Re-Armament the Basic Answer."

Robert Schuman acknowledges this force in Franco-German relations.

The Socialist, for six years Mayor of Milan, says, "Moral Re-Armament is the only arm by which no one is conquered and all are conquerors."

General Ho Ying-chin, who was Commander-in-Chief of the Chinese Armies, spoke recently in the Upper House of the Japanese Parliament. He said, "Moral Re-Armament is the only basis for lasting peace for China and Japan. It is priority."

This world-wide advance is in process of mighty development. A book, *The World Rebuilt*, which appears in twenty countries and ten languages, is eagerly read by all and is understandable by all.

Only last January I said in my statement to the press, "The airlines will lead the way." The fact that five delegations from the airlines with special planes are attending this Assembly shows how wonderfully this guidance is being fulfilled. A few days ago Captain Eddie Rickenbacker, speaking to 2500 of his employees in Eastern Air Lines, said, "Unless we grow morally, mental and financial growth won't last. If you and I can take the one fundamental principle of Moral Re-Armament, honesty, and live up to that, the other three will follow. Our ambition is to build leadership of the quality Moral Re-Armament is teaching. If everyone of us could overnight put this spirit into action it would guarantee America would be sure to survive."

My deep personal wish is to have every American free under the direction of God to fight for America; so to fight that America really be free, free from the tyranny of sin, under God's direction—the unseen but ever-present Power. I wish this no less deeply for everyone in every nation. I don't want our sons, especially our fighting sons, to go about without an answer. It simply enslaves them. It is not good enough. It will drive them to the same philosophy that rules our opponents. We shall never create an inspired democracy that way. Men must learn to have a faith that will create the right revolution. If we can spread this revolution fast enough we can save America and the world. Unless we have this revolution there will be a revolution of chaos.

It needs this stronger dose. Sin leaves us with such a dull, heavy thud. "The blood of Jesus Christ His Son cleanseth us from all sin." That is the discovery everyone is looking for. That is the answer.

Then you will have a wonderful example that the whole world will want to follow. You will have an America to which the wise and honest can repair. And that is what the world expects today of America. You will have a battle cry of freedom, and that is what America wants. You will have a democracy that is really inspired.

Then our young men and our old men will fight as Lincoln fought of old. Our young men will know what to fight for and our wars will be won. And we shall be at peace with all men and the whole world.

6. THE FORGOTTEN FACTOR

•

The world premiere of *The Forgotten Factor* took place in the National Theatre, Washington, in May 1944, under the sponsorship of a national committee whose co-chairmen were Senator Harry S. Truman and Representative James W. Wadsworth of New York. At a previous showing for industrialists and labor leaders in Philadelphia, Senator Truman and Representative Wadsworth addressed the audience after the performance:

SENATOR TRUMAN:

I have been rather overwhelmed by the lessons that are so capably demonstrated in this play we have just witnessed. This country is at the crossroads for the greatest future that any nation in the world has ever faced. Or disaster. Whichever we want to make it.

My experiences of the last two and a half years have given me somewhat of an insight into human nature as it works under stress and strain. We can't operate as the greatest Republic in the world without trusting the other fellow, and he has got to give us reason to trust him. That is the thing this group is reawakening in us—that fundamental pioneer spirit which caused this country to grow and become as great as it is now.

You in Philadelphia have a tremendous opportunity. If you leaders will take this spirit of Moral Re-Armament and put it to work with everything you've got, you could demonstrate the answer that the whole country is looking for.

I wish I were thirty years younger to see this thing work out. I know it is going to. I wish I could come back in two generations and see the greatest country in all the history of the world.

(America today needs fundamental moral truth.) We have seen it brilliantly and entertainingly presented tonight. I sincerely hope that we will all take it to heart and spend more time reading the twentieth chapter of Exodus and the fifth, sixth, and seventh chapters of St. Matthew, and living out the lesson given us in this room. It would make the world a very different place, (the world we all want.)

REPRESENTATIVE WADSWORTH:

Fellow Americans, I have tremendous faith in this movement. It is a faith that comes to me instinctively. I have read the commendations written and spoken by men of tremendously wide experience in the industrial field, both on the side of Management and of Labor. I have seen it at work in the addresses made this evening and in this remarkable play. I confess to you that it reaches very, very deep down in the heart, this play.

This country of ours is faced with a tremendous crisis. The crisis is not tapering off. The going will be tougher before it is easier—tougher in casualties, tougher in the way of sacrifice, in the demands made upon us all on what we call the home front. It is going to strain all our strength and demand all our spirit. We shall do the task so infinitely better if we do it together, hand in hand, trusting one another, having faith in one another through intimate contact. Moral Re-Armament is teaching us that.

The crisis, so far as our institutions in this country are concerned, will not end with victory on the field of battle. New difficulties will confront us—complications extraordinary. And if men do not work together with each other, but work apart, distrusting each other, we may tear down everything that we hold sacred in this country after we have defeated our country's enemies.

Yes, we do have difficulties ahead. I, for one, am grateful for the inspiration these people have given me—and I know they have given you—the inspiration that will lead us to gird our loins for the conflicts that are coming, and the inspiration to fight these conflicts side by side as Americans.

> Since 1944 *The Forgotten Factor* has played to audiences totaling 250,000 in the United States; 200,000 in Britain; 120,000 in Germany; 100,000 in South Africa; 36,000 in Norway, Sweden, and Denmark; 35,000 in Switzerland; 32,000 in New Zealand; 30,000 in France; 27,000 in Finland; 25,000 in Canada; 8,000 in Australia.
>
> Typical of the many invitations was that from New Zealand in 1949 from five cabinet ministers of the present and five cabinet ministers of the retiring government and other leading citizens. The Hon. F. W. Doidge, Minister of External Affairs, speaking at a performance in Wellington, said on February 21, 1950:

The world is really at war—a conflict terrifying and inescapable. It is the fight between good and evil, and that is the theme of the play—the war for the minds of men.

The aim of Moral Re-Armament is to fill the ideological vacuum. In this fight we face a vital truth. This is not merely a war for power but for men's minds and souls.

In that war, if we are to save the world, we have to realize that Moral Re-Armament is more important than the atom bomb.

7. A COMMUNIST'S TEN POINTS

•

Mr. Max Bladeck, Works Council Chairman in the
Rheinpreussen Coal Mining Company, Moers, Ger-
many and for twenty-one years a member of the
Communist Party, made the following statement at
Caux in July 1950:

I want to tell you why I, a
former Communist, am now a fighter for MRA. Here are
some of my reasons:

1. Moral Re-Armament puts people before things.

2. It brings people together in Germany and in the whole
world and can bring a new age of justice. It is the only ideology in which people of all religions and all confessions can
come together on the basis of the four absolute moral standards.

3. It gives to each person in a democracy a sense of responsibility.

4. It is not anti-anything, and from the two opposing sides,
management and labor, it develops the positive forces and
unites them in the way which is in the best interests of the
workers and of the whole country.

5. It puts every statesman who lives according to these
principles above party and enables him to work for the good
of all the people.

6. Moral Re-Armament is the only ideology which does
not set man against man but shows how to win enemies by
love, and in this way it fights for world peace.

7. It gives to every nation a political and economic plan
which can produce a new era of peace and real happiness for
mankind.

8. This ideology, if it is accepted by people, will prevent
war and therefore will preserve the basic life of humanity and

its culture. It will fight with everything it has to produce the right development and progress of humanity.

9. It creates sound family life and, beyond that, sound national life and a sound world.

10. It knows no foreigners. It brings all races and all classes together in the unity of goodwill and makes them into a real united nations of the heart.

Do you know any ideology that can do more than that? That is why I fight with all my faith and all my strength for this ideology.

8. THE GESTAPO REPORT

•

The Gestapo report, *Die Oxfordgruppenbewegung*, was compiled in 1942 by the Head Office of the Reich Security Department. The discovery of this 126-page document during the German retreat from France was first disclosed in an Associated Press dispatch by the distinguished American columnist, DeWitt Mackenzie. On December 29, 1945, the following letter appeared in *The London Times:*

Christianity in Germany

A NAZI DOCUMENT

SIR,

Nazi Germany's determination to destroy Christianity has been apparent for many years, but nowhere has it been more categorically stated than in a secret Gestapo report which has now been discovered. As this document has received less attention than it deserves, we trust that you will allow us to set some brief extracts before your readers.

The document, which, as its title page states, was prepared by the head office of the Reich Security Department, concerns

Dr. Buchman and the Oxford Group. It denounces them for "uncompromisingly taking up a frontal position against National Socialism" in that "they encourage their members to place themselves fully beneath the Christian Cross and to oppose the cross of the swastika with the Cross of Christ, as the former seeks to destroy the Cross of Christ." "Frankly, the importance of the Group lies here," the document continues. "At the very moment when we (the Nazi Party) are making efforts to suppress Christian conviction of sin, which appears to us the first step towards the enslavement of the German, a movement is emanating from the Anglo-Saxons, who are racially related to us, which regards just this consciousness of sin as a basis for change in national relationships."

The document further states that the secret police regarded the movement as "the pacemaker of Anglo-American diplomacy" and as a force working "to bring about new political and ideological conditions in the Reich." "The Group as a whole," it says, "constitutes an attack upon the nationalism of the State and demands the utmost watchfulness on the part of the State. It preaches revolution against the National State, and has quite evidently become its Christian opponent."

Speaking of the influence of the campaign for moral rearmament the report continues:

"If one considers the names of the chief propagandists for Buchman's call to moral re-armament in England and elsewhere, the political counterpart of the movement becomes plain: the Jewish Western democracies. Nor is there any room for doubting against whom this whole campaign was directed, bearing in mind the year in which it took place, 1938, the year when—as it was said—Germany attacked little Austria with brutal force. . . . The Group breathes the spirit of Western democracy. It supplies the Christian garment for world democratic aims. The Group and the democracies supplement each other and render each other's work fruitful."

The whole report throws an interesting light on the Nazi mind, as well as finally dispelling the widespread misrepresentations which have been circulated about this Christian movement. We hope that a full translation will be made available to the British public. For it is vital that we should understand the spiritual foundations of democracy as clearly as did our enemies, and that we should sustain with all our strength what they feared and hoped to destroy.

This letter was signed by:

Lord Ammon, Labour Peer and a former Chairman of the London County Council; Harold Clay, then Chairman of the London Labour Party; Lord Courthope, then President of the Union of Conservative Associations of Great Britain; the Bishop of Litchfield, Dr. Edward Woods; Sir Lynden Macassey, then Chairman of Reuters; Sir Cyril Norwood, then President of St. John's College, Oxford; Sir David Ross, then Provost of Oriel College, Oxford, and recently Vice-Chancellor of Oxford University.

9. MILLIONS READY

●

At the time of the visit of *The Forgotten Factor* in Bremen, the following leading editorial appeared in the Bremen paper *Weser Kurier*, February 6, 1950, written by the editor-in-chief, Felix von Eckardt:

The presence of the Moral Re-Armament group in Bremen, and the performances of the industrial play *Der Vergessene Faktor*, have found an echo in all the vital intellects of our city, that has by far exceeded the expectations of the skeptics. So what has happened in other cities has been repeated in Bremen. Whatever your point of view, negative or positive, no doubt can be left that through Moral Re-Armament the people have been touched by something for which they have long been waiting.

There is in the millions a latent readiness to devote themselves to a great uplifting idea; to direct their goodwill for an aim; to give their life and work a meaning without which they cannot carry on their existence. They know also that mortal danger hovers over them, and that trying to meet the danger by material means alone is very questionable.

The people of Caux understand this situation. The danger that threatens Christian culture and thus Europe and all countries whose spiritual origin is in Europe, is not primarily dependent upon the means of power mobilized by the Communists, nor upon tanks, planes, and atom bombs, but upon people who have themselves subscribed to the Communist ideology. Indeed the latter as idealists have a claim to the respect even of those who think otherwise.

Because millions know this danger, or in any case feel it unconsciously, they are not wholly reassured nor given a feeling of inner security by the might of the Western democracies, even though this might is so immense as to lend a sense of outward security.

Why does not the power of the West reassure or, when it does, only partially? Because the inner foundation of real power is lacking, the ideology to which material power is subordinate; the ideology that in extreme emergency even gives the use of force a moral justification. . . .

We have said that millions of people today lack something, since democracy without an ideological basis loses itself in outward mechanics which cannot satisfy man, nor free him from fear, nor give him the capacity for sacrifice. Moral Re-Armament supplies this lack by giving the democratic system a moral foundation.

Caux has set itself to the task of filling the Christian teaching with new lifeblood; of plunging into the middle of the problems of our time; saying to man that the changing of men and systems must always begin with man himself, that we must free ourselves from hatred and mistrust, that the road to reconciliation between the millions starts not with putting a moral challenge to your neighbor but with putting it to yourself, because only by your personal example can you decisively affect the world around you.

Beliefs that come from inner conviction do not lose their value when someone rejects them as "old."

The people of MRA do not try to answer this argument by theoretical discussion. They prove the durability of their ideology by living it. Their world influence can be traced far beyond the expectations of so-called "realist" politicians, and it is this that gives them the happy inner certainty of being on the right road. Innumerable men and women who know the danger that threatens Christendom will follow on this road, because today the durability of the Caux movement is no longer an illusion but a reality.

10. A QUESTION OF CHANGING MEN

•

The Foreword by M. Robert Schuman, French Minister of Foreign Affairs, to the French edition of Dr. Frank Buchman's speeches, published in 1950, reads as follows:

The editors of these speeches have decided to entrust the writing of the preface to a man in political life, a Cabinet Minister in office. We have to admit, however, that thus far statesmen have been only moderately successful in "remaking the world." The fact remains that it is their duty, more than anyone else's, to apply themselves to this task; and it is to their advantage to welcome every assistance offered to them.

If we were being presented with some new scheme for the public welfare or another theory to be added to the many already put forward, I should remain skeptical. But what Moral Re-Armament brings us is a philosophy of life applied in action.

It does not claim to have invented a new system of morals. For the Christian, the moral teaching of Christianity is enough, and he draws from it all the principles which must guide his life as a man and as a citizen.

What we do need, and what is quite new, is a school where, by a process of mutual teaching, we can work out our practical behavior toward others; a school where Christian principles are not only applied and proven in the relationships of man to man, but succeed in overcoming the prejudices and enmities which separate classes, races, and nations.

To begin by creating a moral climate in which true brotherly unity can flourish, overarching all that today tears the world apart—that is the immediate goal.

The acquisition of wisdom about men and their affairs by bringing people together in public assemblies and personal encounters—that is the means employed.

To provide teams of trained men, ready for the service of the state, apostles of reconciliation and builders of a new world, that is the beginning of a far-reaching transformation of society in which, during fifteen war-ravaged years, the first steps have already been made.

It is not a question of a change of policy; it is a question of changing men. Democracy and her freedoms can be saved only by the quality of the men who speak in her name.

That is what Dr. Buchman expresses in simple and moving words. He has declared war on materialism and individualism, twin generators of our selfish divisions and social injustices.

May he be heard and followed more and more, in all nations of the world, by those who today still clash in fratricidal hatred.

> While Prime Minister of France, in 1948, M. Schuman sent the following message to the Tenth Anniversary Assembly for Moral Re-Armament:

Governments are at grips with grave and difficult material problems of feeding, production, wages, and prices. They see peace between nations endangered by the prejudices of race and by the rivalry of conflicting interests. Inside nations people are seeking the reconciliation of liberty with authority and an understanding between the classes. I salute in Moral Re-Armament one of the protagonists of inspired democracy which is destined to re-establish the supremacy of all the spiritual values at the heart of our tormented humanity.

11. I WELCOME YOUR PLAN

•

> The following is the text of a letter from Dr. Konrad Adenauer, Chancellor of the West German Republic, to Dr. Frank Buchman welcoming the plan to hold a demonstration of Moral Re-Armament at Whitsun, 1950, in the Ruhr:

DEAR DR. BUCHMAN,

Moral Re-Armament, which you created and for which you conceived the plan in Germany when you were staying in Freudenstadt, has become universally known in post-war Germany. I think of the great success which the team of Moral Re-Armament has achieved with *The Forgotten Factor* in the Ruhr. As a result of it, extensive circles in politics, business, and labor have come into contact with the idea of Moral Re-

Armament. Furthermore, numerous leading statesmen, leaders of the trade unions and of industry and commerce have followed the invitation to take part in the annual conferences at Caux. They were grateful for the opportunity which Caux offered to discuss the urgent problems of Germany on a world basis and in an atmosphere of wholehearted co-operation with representatives from all the nations in which personal liberty is guaranteed.

I believe that in view of the offensive of totalitarian ideas in the East of Germany, the Federal Republic, and within it the Ruhr, is the given platform for a demonstration of the idea of Moral Re-Armament. I therefore welcome your plan to hold a conference and a public demonstration of Moral Re-Armament at Whitsun in the Ruhr, to which delegates would be invited from all parts of the world.

With best regards, I am,

Yours very truly,

Adenauer

Simultaneously, Herr Karl Arnold, Minister-President of North Rhine-Westphalia and then President of the Bundesrat, extended to Dr. Frank Buchman the following invitation:

The work of Moral Re-Armament has proved through the years that it is capable of awakening new creative forces in Germany and Europe. From the reports I have received I am convinced that the demonstration and conference which Moral Re-Armament plans to hold in the Ruhr will be especially well calculated to achieve further success on the road you have pioneered.

I would be most happy if it would be possible for you to come to Germany during these days. I therefore have the honor of extending to you a warm invitation to come here and I know that the heads of several Land Governments welcome the proposal and plan to take part in the events.

Arnold

Statement to the Press issued from the office of the
President of the Bundesrat, Herr Karl Arnold, Bonn,
May 19, 1950.

It is in view of the extreme urgency of the European and
world situation and of the unique position of Germany between East and West, that the Federal Chancellor and the
President of the Bundesrat are taking the initiative in welcoming a public demonstration of Moral Re-Armament at Whitsun in the Ruhr.

The idea of Moral Re-Armament is not new in Germany.
Two years ago all the Minister-Presidents of the German
Länder in the British and American zones, in a joint telegram
to Dr. Buchman on his seventieth birthday, described this ideology as "the indispensable foundation for peace and the reconstruction of Europe and the world."

Since then Moral Re-Armament has become universally
known throughout this country; one hundred and forty thousand Germans in twenty-four cities, representing all parties,
classes, and professions, have seen the ideological plays, *The
Good Road* and *The Forgotten Factor*. This past winter *The
Forgotten Factor* has been presented in Hamburg and Bremen
by invitation of the Lord Mayors and Senates of those two
cities, and during recent weeks it has been shown to audiences
totalling twenty-five thousand in the Ruhr, centering at Gelsenkirchen.

Those who have invited Dr. Buchman to Germany at this
time believe that the entire international situation could
change overnight if proof were given that Europe possessed
the force for a new life. The purpose of these Whitsun events,
in the industrial heart of Europe, is to provide this proof by
demonstrating a basis of ideological unity for the nation which
is a decisive battleground in the world war of ideas.

12. IDEOLOGY IN THE PITS

•

The following editorial appeared in the *Stoke-on-Trent City Times* on June 18, 1948:

What are the North Stafford-shire miners after?

What brought India's Postmaster-General and Bombay's Minister of Labour to our coalfields within the space of a few weeks? Why have coal-face miners from North Staffordshire been invited by responsible statesmen to America and half a dozen Continental countries? Is it just because of their increasing production, or have they an invisible export that nations need even more than coal?

Now we hear that our miners are holding a national rally for Moral Re-Armament in the Victoria Hall, Hanley, under the slogan, *Europe—The Miners' Answer*.

To this they have invited mining delegations from every British coalfield, and from the coalfields of Northern France, Belgium, Holland and the Ruhr.

Exporting an Answer

Is this just another production drive—a boost for the National Coal Board?

Heaven knows we need that; but in our opinion our miners are after something much, much bigger than that. They are beginning to export not only coal, but something which the democracies need more than anything else to-day—an inspired ideology.

It is over eighteen months now since almost any Saturday afternoon on Stoke Station you could have seen parties of miners and their wives boarding the 3.18 train for London.

To have seen them return you would have had to stay up into the small hours of Sunday morning, when a special bus would bring them back from Crewe, depositing them, tired but happy, at their homes all over North Staffordshire.

Where had they been to, and who was paying for them?

They had travelled at their own expense to the Westminster Theatre, where *The Forgotten Factor*, Moral Re-Armament's industrial play, drew crowded houses from October to April, all through that terrible winter.

Altogether more than 300 of them saw it during that time. So it was hardly surprising that the cast of *The Forgotten Factor* received a pressing invitation from the National Union of Mineworkers and from colliery officials in North Staffordshire. They interrupted their successful run in London for a week in the Potteries. More than 7,000 people poured into the Queen's Hall, Burslem, for the five performances.

A New Incentive

Soon, from many pits in this area, came first-hand evidence of increased production, better teamwork between management and labour, a new incentive, and the answer to subversive forces in the industry.

At one North Staffordshire pit it was said that the undermanager would rather meet the Devil himself at the coalface than the Union Branch Secretary.

The Forgotten Factor made such a difference that they are now able to work things out together.

Recently there have been long drawn-out negotiations about prices on a new coalface, which always ended in deadlock. The Branch Secretary says, "We took an unprecedented step for North Staffordshire, and asked Coal Board and management representatives to our monthly union meeting. Discussing the matter on a basis of what's right and not who's right, we reached agreement."

A union secretary's wife says that since her husband saw

The Forgotten Factor, fifteen months ago, their home life has been so much happier that she has fallen in love with him all over again.

Soon enough our miners realised that here was a secret they could and must export. They took the Westminster Theatre one Saturday night, and invited every pit consultative committee in Britain to *The Forgotten Factor*.

The theatre was crowded with miners and their families from all over the coalfields. Since then 150 pits have asked for the play to be brought to their areas. It has played in Warwickshire, Leicestershire, Cannock Chase, North Wales and South Wales coalfields, and before industrial audiences in Wolverhampton and Birmingham.

In all these areas North Staffordshire miners have introduced the play, often travelling long distances after their day's work, and returning home the same night to be ready for the next shift at the coalface.

Coalface to Congress

When American Congressional Committees visited Europe to make recommendations for Marshall Aid, they specially asked to meet miners from North Staffordshire and other coalfields where Moral Re-Armament is at work. One of our men from the coalface—Mr. Bill Yates—visited America last Christmas. He created such an impression there that he was recently invited to return by a Committee of Senators and Congressmen to speak at the World Assembly for Moral Re-Armament in California.

Another spoke at a great gathering of miners and factory workers at Wuppertal in the Ruhr, and yet another introduced *l'Élément Oublié*, the French version of *The Forgotten Factor*, to the miners of Lille and Lens.

Others have visited Switzerland, Norway, Sweden, Denmark and Holland, and have told Cabinet Ministers, industrialists and labour leaders in those countries what is happening in North Staffordshire.

Where does the money come from for all this? You may well ask. Air and sea travel, and even rail travel, are expensive these days, and time costs money too. Some months ago the miners themselves got together and decided to start a Fighting Fund to which anyone could contribute to send their spokesmen wherever the needs of the world and their burning conviction should lead them.

Some have gone without their smokes and drinks, others have sold cherished possessions, and thousands have shared in the privilege of sacrifice for a great cause.

The personnel manager of a Black Country factory summed it up in this way: "The industrial revolution which started here changed the face of the world; the new revolutionary force of *The Forgotten Factor* will change its heart."

13. HOPE FOR THE FUTURE

•

The following statement was issued by Mr. Henry Ford, founder of the Ford Motor Company, in connection with the nationwide MRA campaign of 1939:

The objective of Moral Re-Armament is one in which I strongly believe. It stands for an attitude and an effort that is deeply needed in all the seats of public and private power today. As plain people, it seems to me, we have stronger and more healthy moral convictions than ever before. The majority of human beings are normally honest, kind, sane-minded, and industrious, building their world around home and children, and desiring more than anything else the blessings of peace, good order, and fair dealing.

The effort of the Oxford Group, under the leadership of Dr. Frank N. D. Buchman, to bring into high places the honesty and humanity of common life is what I understand "Moral Re-Armament" to mean and that effort I cordially endorse. There is enough good will in the people to overcome all war, all class dissension, and all economic stagnation, when that good will shall be hitched to the affairs of men and nations. This is the one kind of power in which governments of men are deficient and of the usability of which they seem unaware. A movement that translates our private moral convictions into our public policies appeals to all who would help the world forward to its next stage of progress. Moral Re-Armament gives me hope for the future of our country and the world, because of the results that are being achieved.

14. THE DILEMMA OF LABOR

•

The following article by Mr. Robert Edwards, General Secretary of the British Chemical Workers' Union and Chairman of the International Committee of the Socialist Movement for the United States of Europe, is taken from the *Southern Cross*, Wellington, the only Labour daily newspaper in Australasia, dated August 30, 1950:

One of the most significant features in recent years is the influence Moral Re-Armament has had, and is having, on the whole of the Labour and Trade Union Movement of the world. During recent weeks, many well-known leaders of world Labour have found themselves impelled to visit Caux, Switzerland, and to discover there the great experiment in equality and practical Socialism that they have been aspiring to achieve throughout their lives.

The great new revolutionary force of MRA will have increasing influence on world Labour, because it has the answer to Labour's dilemma in every country. The Labour Movement was founded by men and women who dedicated themselves to build a new civilisation where co-operation would replace competition, where men and women would win freedom and security, and where the nations of the world would be united in the spirit of freedom and peace.

The pioneers of the Labour Movement, many of whom professed to be materialists and atheists, were, in fact, men of great religious fervour.

They understood the need for personal example and self-sacrifice, but as Labour has moved into power in many countries and toward power in others, this spirit of sacrifice and religious fervour has disappeared. The process within the Labour Movement can be summed up in four words—sacrifice, struggle, success and then stagnation.

The stagnation can be attributed to failure to deal with moral and ethical questions. We have been concerned with political and economic arguments, not with the fundamental necessity of personal change in the individual.

A mighty force, that should have captured the world and built a new civilisation, has lost impetus and is being overwhelmed by the materialistic onslaught of Russian Communism.

My first visits to the USSR, which began when I headed the youth delegation there in 1926, and met all the leaders from Trotsky to Stalin and Molotov, led me to believe that here was a social experiment that might well produce a great new civilisation, and prove itself a strong arm for peace.

Later, I was to be disillusioned and forced to look elsewhere for the answer to Labour's dilemma. This I have found at Caux.

While I was at Caux, the news of the tragic conflict in Korea burst on the world, a conflict which could involve humanity in a devastating atomic war.

Why is it that, after the tremendous sacrifice of life and wealth in a war for democracy, great military victories are turning into bitter defeats? Western democracy can win military victories, but they are not enough. You cannot impose governments on people; you can only educate people to elect their own governments, in which they can believe and place their trust.

This is not a question of institutions or organisations; it is fundamentally a moral issue that can only be decided in men's hearts by the strength of their faith and convictions.

In Eastern Europe, as in Korea, we have witnessed the advance of totalitarian materialism that has swept aside the governments of country after country as if they never existed. In many cases, the forces of Communism have been assisted by the willing help of millions of working people who have lost faith in Western democracy. They lost faith because they feel that the churches preach Christianity but do not practise it, that politicians are seeking personal gain, and that the West has failed to offer a realistic alternative to totalitarian Communism capable of inspiring the masses.

The common peoples of the world have very simple demands.

The common people want a new civilisation where youth can enjoy the springtime of life, where the universities of the world are open to the children of the common people, where the institutions of culture, no longer the private monopoly of the rich, can be used as a link between nations. They want a civilisation where men and women can enjoy a happy, adventurous, carefree life.

This is the world the revolutionary ideas of Moral Re-Armament as striving to achieve.

15. WORLD INDUSTRIAL CONFERENCE, JUNE 1950

•

The 1950 World Assembly at Caux opened with a special conference sponsored by a distinguished group of industrialists and trade unionists. They stated in their invitation:

Political, industrial and labour leaders to-day are facing problems that baffle human wisdom. The technical problems of an industrial age are now complicated by the cross currents of an ideological age.

No one group, no one class, no one nation or race is adequate to solve our problems and to change the course of the world away from unemployment, poverty and war towards an age of security and prosperity.

This will take the combined efforts of all, plus a wisdom greater than that of the most brilliant individuals.

The Conference of Moral Re-Armament at Caux has become the magnet that has drawn together leaders from eighty-two nations to learn the secret and hear the evidence of a positive ideology at work uniting and remaking the world. Men with years of experience in statesmanship and industry, of every political colour, from management and labour, of every faith and no faith, have been finding in Caux the missing key to the problems of the ideological age in which we live.

We, therefore, invite you to join us at Caux to see at first-hand this evidence from Ruhr industries, British coalfields and docks, from Italian, French, and Swiss industrial plants, from Belgium, from Holland, Scandinavia, Australasia and the United States of America, evidence of an answer to the ideological problems besetting world industry.

The men and women responsible for these practical achievements will tell the successive steps that have led to change in their industrial and political situations.

Spokesmen from Africa, India, and Pakistan, the Near and Far East, who have seen national and ideological aspirations find a positive, constructive direction, will report fully on this aspect of the world programme of Moral Re-Armament.

In a critical hour for mankind Caux demonstrates an overarching ideology for East and West, for Left and Right, for Management and Labour.

ANGELO COSTA
President of the Confederation of Italian Industry.

HOWARD COONLEY
Director and Past President of the National Association of Manufacturers, United States.

GEORGES VILLIERS
President of the National Council of French Employers.

SIR JOHN CRAIG
Chairman of Colville's Ltd., Steel Manufacturers, Great Britain.

OTTO SPRINGORUM
Chairman of the Gelsenkirchen Coal Mining Company, Germany.

ICHIRO ISHIKAWA
President of the Federation of Economic Organisations of Japan.

HUSSEIN BEY FAHMY
Former Minister of Finance, Director of the Egyptian Federation of Industries.

N. H. TATA
Director Tata Industries, India.

C. N. McKAY
President of the Associated Chambers of Manufacturers of Australia.

EVERT KUPERS
President, Dutch Confederation of Trade-Unions, 1928–40, 1945–48; Chairman of the Trade Union Advisory Committee for the European Recovery Programme.

PAUL FINET
Secretary-General of the General Federation of Labour, Belgium; President of the International Confederation of Free Trade Unions.

ANDREW NAESMITH
Member of the General Council of the British Trades Union Congress; General Secretary of the Amalgamated Weavers' Association.

TOM YATES
Member of the General Council of the British Trades Union Congress; General Secretary, National Union of Seamen; Member, Management Committee of the International Transport Workers Federation.

DAVID J. McDONALD
Secretary-Treasurer, United Steelworkers of America; C.I.O. Member of the General Council, International Confederation of Free Trade Unions.

QUINTO QUINTIERI
Vice-President of the Confederation of Italian Industry.

ANDRÉ WALLAERT
President of the Employers' Federation of Northern France.

F. Q. DEN HOLLANDER
President of the Board of Management of the Netherlands Railways.

HISATO ICHIMADA
Governor of the Bank of Japan.

RYUTARO TAKAHASHI
President of the National Chamber of Commerce of Japan.

C. S. MACLEAN
President of the Transvaal Chamber of Mines, 1945–46 and 1948–49.

HANS BILSTEIN
Chairman of the Employers' Association of the German Metal Industry.

ROBERT CARMICHAEL
President of the Jute Industry of France.

CHRISTIAN HARHOFF
President of the Danish Shipowners' Association.

LUIZ D. VILLARES
President of the Elevadores Atlas S.A., Brazil.

HANS DÜTTING
General Director, Gelsenkirchen Group, Gelsenkirchen Coal Mining Company.

ERNST KUSS
Director-General of the Duisburg Copper Works, Germany.

ROBERT DURRER
Professor of Metallurgy, Swiss Federal Institute of Technology.

THEO GOLDSCHMIDT
President of the Chamber of Commerce of Essen, Germany.

KHANDUBHAI DESAI
President of the Indian National Trades Union Congress.

R. BROADBY
Secretary of the Australian Council of Trade Unions.

A. W. CROSKERY
President of the New Zealand Federation of Labour.

KOMAKICHI MATSUOKA
Chairman of the National Federation of Labour of Japan.

HARIHARNATH SHASTRI
General Secretary of the Indian National Trades Union Congress.

OH SIEN HONG
President of the Indonesian Federation of Labour.

GASTON TESSIER
President of the French Confederation of Christian Workers; President of the International Confederation of Christian Trade Unions.

KHOSROV HEDAYAT
Secretary of the Iranian Trade Unions; President, Asian Federation of Labour.

PAUL VISSER
President of the Mine Workers' Union of South Africa.

ERNST SCHARNOWSKY
President of the Organization of Independent Trade Unions of Greater Berlin.

ETSUO KATO
Chairman of the National Railway Workers' Union, Japan.

PIERRE-AUGUSTE COOL
President of the Confederation of Christian Trade Unions, Belgium.

KEN BAXTER
Secretary of the New Zealand Federation of Labour.

ALBERT SCHÄFER
President of the Chamber of Commerce of Hamburg, Germany.

HASSAN NACHAT PASHA
Vice-President of the Egyptian Federation of Industries.

MARTIN SCHWAB
Managing Director of the Telefunken Electrical Company, Germany.

FRITS PHILIPS
Vice-President, Philips Radio, Holland.

FRIEDRICH ALFRED SPRINGORUM
Technical Director, Hüttenwerke Huckingen (Mannesmann Steel), Germany.

BJARNE ERIKSEN
Managing Director of the Norwegian Hydro-Electric Power Company.

SIR ROY PINSENT, BART.
Birmingham.

W. N. PERRY
Dominion President of the Federated Farmers of New Zealand.

RUDOLF HUBER
Manager, Oerlikon Machine Works, Switzerland.

SIR J. A. C. ALLUM
President of the Auckland Employers' Association; Mayor of Auckland, New Zealand.

DR. GÖSTA EKELÖF
Founder of the National Training Institute for Industries, Sweden.

KJELL LUND
Managing Director of the Sulitjelma Copper Mines, Norway.

FREDERIK SCHELE
Managing Director of Osram, Sweden.

EERO ANTIKAINEN
President of the Farm Workers' Union of Finland; Member of the Executive of the Finnish Trades Union Congress.

CHRISTIAN LARSEN
President of the National Union of General Workers, Denmark.

S. DE A. PEQUENO
President of the Federation of Tramway Workers of Brazil.

JEAN DUCROS
President of the Confédération Générale des Cadres, France.

MAURICE BOULADOUX
Secretary-General of the French Confederation of Christian Workers.

F. CRAIG
National Secretary of the Timberworkers' Union, New Zealand.

R. FREELAND
National Secretary of the Harbour Board Employees' Union, New Zealand.

AUGUST STEFFEN
General Secretary of the Christian Socialist Trade Unions of Switzerland.

F. P. WALSH
Vice-President of the New Zealand Federation of Labour.

L. WESTVIG
National President of the Wood Workers' Union, Denmark.

W. CALDER MACKAY
General Manager of the Farmers' Trading Company Limited, New Zealand.

HEIKKI H. HERLIN
Member of the Executive of the Association of Engineering and Metal Industries, Finland.

16. WORLD LABOR AND CAUX

•

The following Foreword to *World Labour and Caux*,
a report containing the speeches and statements of
Trade Union and Socialist leaders, was written by
Evert Kupers, President, Dutch Confederation of
Trade Unions, 1928–40 and 1945–48; Socialist Member of Parliament, 1929–48; Vice-President, World
Federation of Trade Unions, 1945–49; Member, Pre-
paratory Committee of the International Confederation of Free Trade Unions, 1949; Chairman, Trade
Union Advisory Committee for the European Recovery Programme.

This is no ordinary book. It
contains statements made by a great number of prominent as
well as less known leaders of the Trade Union and Socialist
movements from practically every part of the world. They
underline the importance of the ideology of Moral Re-Armament in our society.

These men have a great record in the fight to raise the material and spiritual standards of life of the working class. Most
of them have felt personally the hardships of a worker's existence, low wages, long working days, bad housing conditions,
lack of social legislation and social security. Against such injustices they have revolted with all their heart and soul. With
complete dedication they have thrown themselves into the
battle to put an end to these wrongs. . . .

Coupled with the material advancement of the workers
there has been spiritual progress. In a number of countries the
Labour Movement has acquired a social and political position
which practically no one would have dreamed of half a century ago.

But even so, something is missing, the lack of which is being
felt by many. That something is a sense of spiritual stability

in this torn world in which there are such alarming divisions between the nations.

Moral Re-Armament says to all people: if you want to make the world better, start with yourself.

The thousands of people who have visited the assemblies at Caux during recent years have been deeply impressed by their message for our age and by the real comradeship and unity which they have found there. And many have expressed these feelings in this book, the reading of which I can most strongly recommend.

Finally, I would like to pay tribute to the great leadership and love of humanity of Dr. Frank Buchman, the pioneer of Moral Re-Armament, who has devoted himself to the task of establishing a sound basis for the progress of mankind. His work has been the inspiration of the Caux assemblies.

Amsterdam, February, 1950   EVERT KUPERS

17. THE NEW PRIORITY FOR INDUSTRY

•

Mr. Ernesto G. Diederichsen, textile manufacturer, Brazil, made the following speech at Caux, in August 1950:

The time has come for management to understand its real function in our times. Its function is to lead industry in the reconstruction of the world, by the light of absolute moral standards. That means inspired leadership, inspired by absolute co-operation between changed management and workers.

Management has to change. We have to change to live out the ideology of Moral Re-Armament. This ideology has three characteristics. First, it is world-wide in scope. Secondly, it makes clear that "as I am, so is my nation, and so is my factory." Thirdly, it shows that there is a plan for each of us, a plan for management, a plan for labor.

The meaning of that plan for myself is, first to realize and live out the responsibility of management. This means we are responsible for the workers as human beings, to the fullest extent. That includes the recognition that men are more important than machines; that workers are human beings and not merely elements of production. My personal opinion is that because management has not recognized its responsibility to the fullest extent, it is responsible for the many hard feelings and the soreness in industrial life. I want, in my name and the name of management, to apologize for this great fault on our part.

So management has to change, and live out its real responsibility. This includes the responsibility for the workers when they are in the factories and when they are out of the factories. We are responsible for the workers' conditions, for their work and wages.

But that is not by any means enough as a program of change for management. Management is also responsible for the ideology of the workers. To promote the living out of the ideology of Moral Re-Armament in industry is the best security management can give to labor. It means creating happy families, who live under the guidance of God, in the light of the absolute moral standards. How can a worker be really efficient when he is not happy at home?

Then there is another question, wages. To be happy at home it is necessary to have absolute moral standards. But you also have to have wages high enough to live on. This will come as a consequence of labor and management living by those absolute moral standards, and by the guidance of God.

Secondly, how can management find and live out the answer to greed? Labor has suffered many times from the greed of management. We have to change now, and live out the ideology of the four absolutes. Labor deserves a just share in the profits, but what amount should it be? That is the great thing. And it will be worked out by teamwork, as we have learnt at Caux, by labor and management working together in an atmosphere of honesty and understanding. This is the answer for greed. Frank Buchman said, "If everyone cared enough and everyone shared enough, wouldn't everyone have enough? There is enough in the world for everyone's need, but not for everyone's greed." A new aim, a new top priority for industry, is now set: it is the remaking of the world.

18. THE WAR-TIME PROGRAM OF MRA

•

From an article in the *Army and Navy Journal*, Washington, May 6, 1944.

"Napoleon's axiom, 'Morale is to material as three is to one' has been upset. The ratio now stands at six to one." This statement of General Marshall's takes on new importance as we make preparations to strike with an invasion force. Our leaders know that to the excellence of arms and training must be added the decisive weapons of heart, mind and will to absorb the shock of battle and carry through to victory.

An important factor in building this fighting spirit on both battle front and home front has been the program of Moral Re-Armament. In a report recently published here, a group of British leaders, political, industrial and military, write: "National strength springs from the spirit of the people. In time of war that spirit is decisive, and it will be no less needed in the years after victory. For this reason we, with large numbers of representative citizens in this country, recognize the vital importance of the work for Moral Re-Armament and believe that they should be given every encouragement in their essential national service. Their work has proved its success in bringing to life for men and women of all classes the great spiritual values which are the fabric of our nation and for which we battle."

The MRA program was outlined for America eight months before Pearl Harbor in terms of sound homes, teamwork in industry and national unity, in a widely read handbook entitled *You Can Defend America*, with a foreword by General Pershing. This was dramatized in a war revue of the same name which in the next year and a half was shown before a quarter of a million people in over twenty states, and which was the spearhead of campaigns to build a war-winning spirit throughout the nation.

Since Pearl Harbor Moral Re-Armament has been credited by competent observers such as Senator Truman and Congressman Wadsworth with increasing war production in many key aircraft plants and shipyards. Senator Truman said of MRA: "They have rendered great assistance to the all-out war program by creating the spirit of cooperation between management and labor, reducing absenteeism, heightening all-round efficiency and increasing production. There is not a single industrial bottleneck I can think of which could not be broken in a matter of weeks if this crowd were given the green light to go full steam ahead."

Maj.-Gen. Francis B. Wilby, Superintendent of the U.S. Military Academy, after inspecting the results of their work on the home front, said: "This is the arm behind the army." Admiral Richard E. Byrd described it as "the fight for a new America, strong, clean and united."

In Britain, which has faced invasion and blitz, MRA has played a distinctive part in toughening the spirit of the people. In the dedication of her war-time best seller of stories of heroism on the home front, *Come Wind, Come Weather*, Daphne du Maurier, author of *Rebecca*, praised MRA's contribution in Britain's hour of crisis, and said: "I want especially to thank an American, Dr. Frank N. D. Buchman, whose initial vision for Moral Re-Armament made possible their work."

During the four and a half years of war, soldiers, sailors and airmen of the United Nations have thronged MRA's training centers in America, England, Canada and Australia. A soldier visiting the London MRA headquarters the other day said, "MRA added a plus to my training. I knew what I was fighting against. Now I know what I am fighting for."

In Norway and other occupied countries Moral Re-Armament has stood up as an unshakeable center of resistance to the Nazi oppression. Though some of its leaders have undergone imprisonment and death, MRA remains a bulwark for a liberated Europe.

We are fighting a war not alone of arms but of ideas. The victor must be strong in both. Cutting through the selfish, soft materialism and moral confusion of the last two decades, MRA has taken the soldierly virtues of discipline, sacrifice and teamwork, of patriotism essential both in war and peace, and applied them fearlessly to home life, industrial and national life. In this battle MRA has cut across and drawn the fire of self-seeking subversive elements and rallied the constructive and patriotic forces in the defense of the nation.

Men who carry the spirit of Moral Re-Armament inspire that fighting faith which General Marshall, after his recent trip round the world, characterized as our greatest need.

19. THE FIRST OBJECTIVE

•

The Prime Minister of Burma, Thakin Nu, sent the following message to Dr. Buchman at the Caux Assembly in 1949:

It gives me much pleasure to send you a message of greeting on the occasion of your conference. A reassessment of our moral values and their application to our problems is a vital necessity today. Discussions which contribute toward such a reassessment will have a beneficial effect on world problems.

The first objective of the people of the world should be to acquire the right conception of life. Although within easy reach of this, they still fail to grasp it because of their indifference. This failure is the main cause of the present world disorder.

The answer will be the same, no matter whether it is for Westerner or Easterner, exploiter or exploited, Christian or non-Christian. It lies in the right conception of life.

To those who have achieved this conception, materialistic objectives which can give only fleeting satisfaction, shorter in duration than the twinkling of the eye, will no longer constitute the main objective. The day when this main objective reassumes its proper place will be the day when real peace will appear in the world. So long as the people of the world do not achieve this realization, neither atomic energy nor ideal resolutions nor endless sermons will bring real peace and unity to humanity.

20. GREATER HISTORY

•

The Prime Minister of East Pakistan, the Hon. Nurul Amin, was the guest of honor at a luncheon held in the London headquarters of MRA, once the home of Clive of India, on August 31, 1950. He said:

Please convey my heartfelt thanks to Dr. Buchman. But for his friends my visits to the European countries would have been a failure.

Dr. Buchman is a great philosopher, and a prophet in that he has foreseen the need of this age. He will live in an abiding place in history because of Moral Re-Armament.

I know that this is an historic house. It belonged to Clive of

India, who conquered Bengal. That was by force of arms. A greater man, Dr. Buchman, whose house this now is, will make greater history not by arms but by a spiritual and moral ideology. I am honored to be welcomed here.

21. FROM CRISIS TO CURE

•

In September 1950, a national committee of eighteen Indian political and industrial leaders, described by one of its members as the most powerful ever to take united action, sent the following invitation to Dr. Frank Buchman to bring an international force of Moral Re-Armament to India:

DEAR DR. BUCHMAN,

Most of us have the pleasure of knowing you and all of us have seen something of the work of Moral Re-Armament, especially in Europe and America.

We are convinced that the true hope for bringing lasting change in social and economic conditions and for bringing peace to the world lies in multiplying such practical results as we believe to have been achieved by Moral Re-Armament— the giving of a new incentive to industry, the change of heart of capitalist and communist alike, the replacing of mistrust, bitterness and hate between individuals and groups with understanding and co-operation.

We consider, therefore, that such moral re-armament of the nations is the need of the hour and the hope of the future.

We agree with you that no one group, no one class, no one nation or race is adequate to solve the problems we are facing to-day or to change the course of the world away from unemployment, poverty and war towards an age of security and prosperity and that this will take the combined efforts of all, plus wisdom greater than that of the most brilliant individuals.

The Father of our country, Mahatma Gandhi, has bequeathed us an unquenchable inspiration to live by the highest ideals, and we are eager for India to play her full part in this noble task.

We would like you to know how glad we would all be to see you in India this winter along with an international team so that we may profit by your experience. Together we must succeed in turning the world from crisis to cure in demonstrating an overarching ideology for Management and Labour, for Left and Right, for East and West.

DR. S. N. AGARWAL
Secretary, Foreign Department
Sarvodaya Samaj, Wardha.

SIR SULTAN AHMED
Former Member of the
Viceroy's Executive Council.

SIR GURUNATH BEWOOR
Managing Director, Air India
Ltd.

THE HON. SHRI CHANDRABHAL
Chairman, Legislative Council,
United Provinces.

SHRI KHANDUBHAI DESAI
President of the Indian National Trades Union Congress.

SIR V. T. KRISHNAMACHARI
Member, National Planning
Commission; Chairman, Fiscal
Commission, 1950.

SHRI G. L. MEHTA
Member, National Planning
Commission.

SIR LAKHSHMANASWAMI MUDALIAR
Vice-Chancellor, Madras
University.

SHRI GULZARILAL NANDA
Deputy Chairman, National
Planning Commission.

SHRI R. K. PATIL
Member, National Planning
Commission.

THE HON. K. M. PATNAIK
Speaker, Legislative Assembly,
Orissa.

SHRI RAMNATH PODAR
Industrialist.

SHRI KRISHNA PRASADA
Director General, Posts and
Telegraphs.

SIR SRI RAM
Former Chairman of the Indian
Chamber of Commerce.

THE HON. DR. B. C. ROY
Chief Minister, West Bengal.

THE HON. DR. SAMPURANAND
Minister of Education, United
Provinces.

THE HON. A. N. SINHA
Minister of Labour, Bihar.

SHRI J. R. D. TATA
Chairman, Tata Industries.

22. ENEMIES BECOME FRIENDS

•

On Saturday, July 29, 1950, the following editorial
appeared in the *New York Times* entitled "Visitors
from Japan":

It is sadly true, among nations
as among individuals, that the friends of yesterday are not
always the friends of today. In compensation, the enemies of
yesterday may not be enemies of today. Vice-President Barkley, receiving a delegation of sixty Japanese officials, businessmen, and labor leaders, could recall a long period of peace and
amity that preceded the recent war and could hope for another such period. Chojiro Kuriyama, member of the Japanese
Diet, could have an attentive hearing as he told the Senate of
his regret for Japan's big mistake and his recognition of American forgiveness and generosity. All this in Washington, D.C.,
on July 28, 1950, a little less than five years after the atomic
bombs fell on Hiroshima and Nagasaki.

One thinks back to 1945 and one thinks ahead to some date
not yet unveiled. To befriend the Japanese now, to hope the
best for them, is not to condone the crimes their leaders committed in their name and with their aid. It is merely to make
clear that peace and goodwill can return, even after the most
terrible events; that though we must continue to hate the evil-
doers—who could without shame forgive the butchers of the
Nazi internment camps?—we know that no nation is beyond
redemption. The word "Russian" has a sinister sound for us
today. In God's good time, when today's shadow has passed
from the world, it may have a pleasing and genial sound.

The mayors of Hiroshima and Nagasaki were among yesterday's visitors. If they felt that they, too, had something to

forgive they had achieved that miracle. For a moment one could see out of the present darkness into the years when all men may be brothers.

23. FOUNDATION FOR A NATION

•

The following message from the Prime Minister of Japan, Mr. Shigeru Yoshida, was conveyed to the 1950 World Assembly at Caux by Mr. Chojiro Kuriyama, a Member of Parliament of the Prime Minister's Party:

I am grateful that seventy-six Japanese delegates who represent various fields have been invited to the MRA World Assembly this year. I would like to express my heartfelt gratitude to Dr. Buchman and his MRA colleagues who are exerting their utmost among the nations in order to remake this suffering world. Japan is expecting a great deal from Moral Re-Armament.

MRA can inspire and give moral content to Japanese democracy by restoring morality which has been at a low ebb since the war.

MRA can inject the nation with a stabilizing force in regard to its ideas and activities by curing rampant materialism.

MRA can build the foundation for a cultured and peaceful nation for the Japanese people who renounced war through the new constitution.

I am confident that these Japanese delegates will bring back the good seed of MRA, and that through the co-operation of MRA friends all over the world the seed will bring forth a great harvest in Japan. Through the Japanese delegation I would like to pay my greatest respects to Dr. Buchman. I have perfect confidence that the Assembly will call forth mighty echoes from the four corners of the world.

24. ALL ASIA WILL LISTEN

•

Before their departure on July 22, 1950, the leaders of the Japanese delegation to the World Assembly for Moral Re-Armament, Mr. Chojiro Kuriyama, representing the Prime Minister's Party, and Mr. Tokutaro Kitamura, formerly Finance Minister, representing the Democratic Party, issued the following statement on behalf of the delegation:

We came to Europe, where Communism began, to find a positive answer to Communism. We found it at Caux, in the ideology of Moral Re-Armament. This way of life is in our opinion the essential basis for a solution to the problems facing us in Asia, and our gratitude goes out to Dr. Frank Buchman and his fellow workers who are its pioneers.

We are also grateful to the people of Europe for the warmth of their welcome. We realize that in the past Japan has caused great suffering to them through her pursuit of false ideas and false roads. We hope in future as a nation to show by our deeds that we have found a change of heart and that we can make our contribution to the remaking of the world.

In our discussions with cabinet ministers in France, Italy, Germany, and Britain, we found an encouraging awareness of the forces at work in the Far East. We welcome this understanding.

In our view far more attention needs to be paid to the ideological side of the democratic concept if this concept is to win Asia. The millions in the Far East must be presented with a philosophy and way of life so appealing that totalitarianism will lose its lure.

Russia has advanced in Asia because the Soviet government

understands the art of ideological war. It fights for the minds of men. We appeal to the governments and peoples of the West to do the same, to make themselves expert in the philosophy and practice of Moral Re-Armament, which is the ideology of the future. Then all Asia will listen.

25. THE GREATEST OF MEMORIES

•

A parliamentary delegation from South Africa, representing the three major political parties attended the World Assembly at Caux in September 1950. The Speaker of the House of Assembly, the Hon. J. F. T. Naudé, addressing the conference said:

Here at Caux I have seen something which changes individuals, nations, and ideologies. I think of Lake Success. Either we must find the way to bring Lake Success to Caux, or Caux to Lake Success. Otherwise we are not going to have any success.

I have had the opportunity to visit Finland, Norway, Sweden, Germany, and Switzerland. The one place where there is happiness, which gives hope for the future, is Caux. After a few years we shall naturally think of the various countries we have visited, but the greatest of those memories will be Caux.

I have been privileged to meet very many people from time to time. I had the great honor of meeting the President of the United States. I have been privileged to meet two Kings of England. I wish to say that the greatest privilege of my life was when yesterday I met Dr. Frank Buchman, a man who has done so much for humanity and given happiness to millions of people. I hope he will be spared a long time to continue in this great work.

MRA has done a lot in our little country. Sixty per cent of

the world's gold is produced there. The result of *The Forgotten Factor* was that when a strike was imminent, *The Forgotten Factor* intervened and the strike was averted. The Chamber of Commerce, the capitalists in our country, and the miners together settled the strike. We are looking forward to this marvelous play, *The Good Road*, coming to South Africa, and I shall not be happy until it does come.

26. THE BRIGHTEST STAR

•

Hon. Karl E. Mundt, Senator from South Dakota and at that time co-chairman of the Smith-Mundt Committee to investigate the United States information program in Europe, wrote as follows in a letter to his constituents sent from Copenhagen in September 1947:

Our Committee paid a visit to Caux, Switzerland, and spent a day and night with the Moral Re-Armament Conference which in some ways comprised the brightest star for the future we have witnessed in all Europe. There we met Dr. Frank Buchman, the sponsor of Moral Re-Armament, and saw the World Premiere of the new dramatic revue, *The Good Road*.

Moral Re-Armament is holding a five months' conference in proverbially neutral Switzerland. Some of its achievements to date are little short of miraculous.

High up in the Alps, this unique force for Good Will is developing a power and a prestige which it was heartwarming to observe. Europe and the world today needs moral revitalization and rearmament more than it needs the arms of war and destruction. No man could attend the conference in Caux and watch the emotions of a new hope light the faces of the people there and not come away convinced that the organized forces of good in this world can defeat the organized forces of evil. It will be no easy contest, but the sacrifices required are small indeed compared to the costs of further conflicts and the consequences of failure.

27. CAUX

•

1. Report to United States Congress

At the beginning of June 1949, the Speaker of the United States House of Representatives, Mr. Rayburn, with the unanimous consent of the House, designated a bi-partisan committee to attend the World Assembly at Caux. The Committee, under the chairmanship of the Hon. Prince H. Preston, Jr., of Georgia, included the Hon. Donald L. O'Toole, of New York; the Hon. Daniel J. Flood, of Pennsylvania; the Hon. George A. Dondero, of Michigan; the Hon. Earl Wilson of Indiana. They arrived at Caux by special military plane on June 4. In the course of his report to the House of Representatives the Chairman of the Committee, Mr. Preston, said (*Congressional Record*, June 21, 1949):

Why has this movement attracted the attention of at least a hundred members of both bodies of Congress? Why did the House send a committee to observe this recent conference? The American press has asked these questions also. I think the answer lies in the fact that this movement has launched a very vigorous campaign to answer Communism in Europe.

That this movement is succeeding in its localized efforts is not disputed. Your committee heard testimonials from labor union presidents, national presidents, and factory owners in which it was admitted that strife and bitter dissension had been replaced by harmony and friendship as a result of the influence of Moral Re-Armament.

Coal-mine operators from the Ruhr Valley and union bosses out of their mines gave testimony to the effectiveness of the plays, *The Good Road* and *The Forgotten Factor*, and acknowledged they had changed their attitude toward the other as a result of the impact of these dramas.

The success of the movement in industrial disputes led Dr. John R. Steelman, former director of the United States Conciliation Service from 1937 to 1944, to say: "It is the most effective single force for industrial conciliation in the country."

Many world figures have praised the efforts of this altruistic group and it is interesting to note the comments of the Department of Justice in a memorandum dated 1st April, 1949, and I quote from it the following: "Moral Re-Armament is a world force having as its principal objective adequate ideological preparedness of free nations for the ideological conflicts in which the world is now engaged, and its objectives are recognized by the Department as worthy and helpful in the strengthening of democratic forces throughout the world."

No force this side of heaven can be felt like the force of inspired humanity marching in unison, moving in harmony with the Cross of Christ as its breastplate and a burning love for freedom urging it on toward a goal, a goal which all of us surely agree must be reached if nations and peoples are to embrace each other and banish war as a means of settling disputes.

Peace is more sought after today than ever before. A more literate world populace is feverishly seeking the answer to the age-old question of how can nations merge themselves into a world family and become as brothers without betrayal. Idealistic as it may seem, it is none the less true that honor and integrity must precede all unifying efforts and these can be attained only when morality and religious influences are permitted to assume their proper roles in the formation of policies and are made a part of the formulas to be applied in the effort.

If this movement is to implement the Marshall Plan and the Atlantic Pact, as Mr. Robert Schuman, Foreign Minister for France, says it will, by establishing an ideology of democracy resting on the premise that the individual is a person of dignity in God's sight, then it is a welcome force, which can be used constructively and well.

2. *Editorial in Catholic Newspaper "Ostschweiz"*

The following article appeared in the Swiss Catholic newspaper *Ostschweiz*, published in St. Gallen, March 10, 1950, entitled *Catholics and Moral Re-Armament*.

In connection with the Instruction "Ecclesia Catholica" of the Holy Office which expressly permits Catholics to participate in mixed confessional meetings for the defense of the fundamental principles of human rights and of religion against the enemies of the Church, or for the rebuilding of the social order, attention should be drawn to a report which the well-known preacher, Father Hugo Lang, O.S.B., gave on the 29th of January in Munich entitled "The Nature and Way of Moral Re-Armament."

Father Lang said in part as follows: "Caux is the headquarters and training center of Moral Re-Armament which has been created by Frank Buchman. It has no intention of being a sect or a religion. It is simply a supernational religious movement which seeks to lead each individual back to the sources of his own religion. This movement of re-awakening sprang from the strong Christian social impulse of its founder. Believe in the goodness of man, live as an example before him, give him the opportunity also to be good—that is the whole magic of Caux. Only when the individual changes, and that is why in Caux just as in the Exercises it is the individual who is dealt with, only so is there hope for renewal of the family, of economic life, of the nation, and of mankind. There are four ideals which are lived out before the individual's eyes in

Caux to inspire and direct him—honesty, purity, unselfishness, and love—not from time to time and conditionally, but eternally and absolutely.

"In my report which I have worked out at the request of a high Church authority, I have purposely emphasized that in Caux those men are at work whom the Pope in his speeches is constantly addressing and calling to work together in the remaking of the world, the men of good will."

The opinion of the Bishop of Lausanne, Fribourg, and Geneva, Monsignor Charrière, is to be noted. According to Father Lang he expressed himself positively about Caux in the following words: "It is not a question whether priests can go to Caux. Priests must go there because Caux calls for the Church and for the priest."

A very valuable article about Moral Re-Armament from the Catholic side comes from the pen of the Director of the "Volkshochschule" in Duisburg, Dr. Bernhard Kaes, Christian Democrat member of Parliament.

Dr. Kaes writes: "The forces which are working together in this movement are aiming to create a real consciousness of what is basic and real. In a secularized world they are aiming to bring to light the buried Christian values. It is not a question of a substitute for religion. It is the determination to act like Christians in the concrete everyday life, to live in the spirit and according to the commands of the Sermon on the Mount and the Gospel. Moral Re-Armament starts from personal perfection as did St. Ignatius when he said: 'If you want to make the world better, begin with yourself.'

"Every genuine, living Christian must be aware that we are living in a pagan world and that Europe has become a mission field. This means that a real movement of the laity is necessary far beyond the boundaries of churches and confessions in order to win ground again for Christianity, and one which fights in a world of widespread militant materialism to re-establish a way of life based on moral and Christian values."

Kaes meets all criticisms of the daily practice of the quiet time (meditation) with the words of the famed French Oratorian priest, Father Gratry, who over a hundred years ago said: "The world will change when each of you changes. We can change by listening to God, for God never ceases to speak to us just as the sun never ceases to shine. Every morning before the distractions and activity of our busy lives begin, we ought to listen to God in a quiet time."

Kaes goes at some length into the concept of ideology, its content, use, and the justification for it in the MRA vocabulary. In contrast to the destructive philosophical ideologies of our time, in contrast to the false religious doctrines and panaceas, Moral Re-Armament is proclaimed as a uniting and superior ideology, or as the battle for a God-inspired ideology. It is easily recognized that the term "ideology" is used in a transcendental sense in contrast to its secularized content and use. What is meant by it is the united mobilization of all effective Christian forces against the seductions of the modern world. . . .

Bernhard Kaes concludes his article with a quotation from Dr. Johannes Aufhauser, Professor at the University of Munich: "In the atmosphere of Moral Re-Armament which is up-to-date in its spirit and broad in its religious feeling, we Catholics can feel ourselves fully at home." He closes his big-hearted statement in these words: "May what I have said find general assent among Catholics, and may we, while recognizing all the necessary cautions that are enjoined on us, be prepared to support and work with these people and be willing at the same time ourselves to take the risk of living out our Christianity."

3. *Some Reflections on the Secret of Caux*

An address by Count Carlo Lovera di Castiglione,
noted Catholic writer and historian, September 1950:

For many years I have been coming to Caux in search of a break in the fevered life of every day; and every year I go back from Caux with a still clearer impression of the strength and help one receives to live one's daily life better.

Where is it that the fruitful secret of Caux really lies? Is it in the four absolutes? In the life one lives? In the example one is given? In the peace and meditation one enjoys? In the people one meets? I have come to the conclusion that the true secret of Caux is in none of these aspects of its life. Its secret lies in the force and example of the evidence and of the way in which it is presented.

All races, all professions, all cultures, all tongues, come one after another on the platform of this hall; and from all these testimonies one gathers an individual and collective experience of life which is arresting in the formidable strength of its example.

Life is present in its most complex reality when we hear workers speaking freely of their situations, of their difficulties, of the misunderstandings to which they are subjected, of their economic misery, of their bitterness. They are no longer just trade union members, but men who at last open their hearts before their own employers. There are employers who speak to us of their experiences in the field of labor, of the force and benefit, not merely moral, which lies in a reconciliation, between workers and employers, and in synchronizing their interests, employers who pass from the economic to the moral plane. There are young nations, emerging from the struggle for their hard-won liberty, who overcome ancient bitternesses. There are races who still wait for justice, and whose voices freely reach other men who belong to the nations which dominate them.

There are men of religion, who tell us of their new-found strength to live better age-old truths which till now seemed out of date or ineffective, just because they were not lived. There are infinite human experiences, sketched in simple, basic lines, in which we often find the elements of our own difficulties, with a practical invitation to overcome them.

Then, too, alongside the secret of the strength of Caux, is

the secret of its charm. Caux is a window open on the world.
It is a crossing of roads which come from every continent.
The workers in particular, who are too often imprisoned in
the monotony of their jobs, of their economy, of their trade
union, they especially appreciate this open window on the
world, and the vast horizons which make them feel more
clearly that longing for greater justice which is felt so deeply
by people everywhere in this terrible modern world. They
learn that this justice cannot be reduced, as historical materialism teaches, to a mere redistribution, to a surgical operation of
cutting and adding, but that it must serve to lift the human
spirit, which is so often oppressed by economic instability,
even though this lifting of the spirit seems almost impossible
for men who live under the burden of daily poverty, lack of
a home, overpopulation, and all the difficulties which lead to
misery, promiscuity, tuberculosis, and degradation in human
life.

This insistence on the dignity of the human person is one
of the "leit-motifs" of Caux. It rightly strikes whoever goes
up to Caux, not merely by the fact of its existence, but because here we see expressed the simplest formula, which can
resolve problems which ideologies and the class war have ter-
ribly and vainly complicated.

This simple formula is always the same: unselfishness, honesty, purity, love. It is adequate for the minor problems of
every day, and for the great social and political problems
which trouble the world.

But in Caux we feel yet another thing: the absence of many
other friends who were once with us, heart to heart: Germans
from the Eastern Zone, Poles, Czechs, Hungarians, Yugoslavs,
proud peoples who were once free and happy, but who today
are oppressed even in the most intimate places of their conscience and of their dignity as men. Some representatives of
these peoples, fugitives from catastrophe, are here with us, as
a painful reminder of the failure of a Europe which has be-
trayed her ancient mission of civilization. Europe today is

threatened by that same ideological materialism which she so light-heartedly and lovingly tended, mistaking it for progress, for a reaction against obscurantism, for peace, for all those things which we as children were so foolishly taught would be eternal gifts. To these people go our thoughts of sympathy today, together with our wishes and our prayers to God for them.

But their absence is a concrete warning which comes from Caux: Remake the world! That is, collect the fragments from the ruins to remake a new home, habitable and welcoming. It is of great comfort that, almost everywhere, the conviction is gaining ground that if to build a house needs bricks, tiles, and mortar, it is even more necessary to have the architect who puts them together for construction. Who will be our architect? The four absolute standards of honesty, purity, unselfishness, and love are this work of architecture. But in order that the architect may build, it is necessary that he know and apply his rules. In the same way, in order that the four standards become operative in remaking the world, they must be lived, even in face of the vain chatterings of the world.

Thus you see how the whole teaching of Caux, how the directives which come in quiet times, the experience and the illuminating power of God which have been given to Frank Buchman, complete one another and fit together with the demand of the individual conscience, from which depends the family conscience, which, in its turn, goes to make up the national conscience; and the world is made up of nations. In Caux there is truly a mission, a challenge to all men to supersede the divisions of class, ideology, and race. "Supersede" is one of the themes of Caux. There is no change without it. Now we, today, have another great conquering force before our eyes. We would be denying light if we were to deny that Communism has positive values and that it is a great totalitarian, conquering force.

But Communism knows what it wants; its followers are capable of great sacrifices, have a great faith, and want to remake the world, enclosing it in an authoritarian, total unity of thought, of discipline, of culture, and of economy.

It is certain that in the Communist dream there is a possibility of renewal and of supremacy. For this very reason their young people, generous as well as intellectual, are launched out as argonauts in search of a new world and of adventure never yet attempted.

But let us be careful that we do not let ourselves be distracted by the height of the building, of which we cannot see the roof. We do not see it because it is missing. Economics and enforced total equality do not resolve the problem. And it is a Marxist Russia herself which proves it.

She, too, has needed, and still needs, a spiritual appeal. To win the war and overcome internal difficulties of every kind, on what did Russia set her values? On spiritual principles formerly denied: honor, patriotism, glory, sacrifice, the spirit of competition, and even, to some extent, proscribed religion.

This is just what is said in Caux: the economic solution does not suffice to remake the world; individuals and nations are only capable of true greatness when they return to moral principles in life, in the family, in their jobs and businesses, in diplomacy, and in politics. Here is true victory over Marxism, which is the inheritance of economic man, but is not the inheritance of the whole man who is made up of spirit and body. This victory does not stand by itself. It is in this relative sphere that MRA is the one solution, inasmuch as it is a modern application, intelligent and active, of the only true solution: a return to Gospel morality. The whole inner strength of Moral Re-Armament is that the spirit of MRA reflects the Spirit of Christ. In this lies the great secret of Caux.

MRA, like all things which tend to put man back into the plan of God, has two sorts of enemies: those who oppose it because they fear it, materialists and the morally defeated. These are its declared enemies; we know them, we do not fear them because we know where and how to fight them. There are other enemies: those who do not understand MRA but presume to judge it. These do much harm, and we must, by showing the application of the principles of MRA in our daily life, fight them, by speaking of MRA in our families, with our friends, with our work mates and office colleagues. We must make them see how it is in reality, without losing ourselves in a labyrinth of details or in discussing superficial aspects of minor importance. That is the favorable ground where our adversaries lie in wait for us. We must propagate and defend the essence of the thinking, of the spirit, of the teaching, and of the effectiveness of MRA in the individual and in the world.

Other enemies of ours are the pessimists. Those who say to us and to others: "What presumption, to remake the world! You?" Well, are we then the only ones who seriously want to remake the world? The Communists, too, seriously want to remake the world! How do they set about it? How do they begin? They begin by means of cells, then various teams. And why should we not do what they can do? Are we not true cells, each one in our own circle, if we truly believe that we have a responsibility for what happens in the world, good and evil? Should we not think seriously of this? Do you not see that there is already a mysterious hand which writes on the wall of Europe "Mene, Tekel, Peres"—"I have weighed you, I have judged you, I have condemned you"? And what sort of Christians will we be if we let the hour pass by? And what sort of intelligence have we if we close our eyes to such obvious reality? And what sort of cowards' hearts have we if we do not know how to love enough in order to act?

These are the questions which concluded my meditation on my stay in Caux. It is for all of us to answer them with faith.

28. THE CHANCE TO SAVE CIVILIZATION

•

Address by Rear Admiral Richard E. Byrd at the conclusion of the New York premiere of *The Good Road*.

This is a most inspiring and in-spired performance. I am much more moved by it than I am willing to admit.

When I think of the thousands of men and women all over the world, old and young, who have left their homes and who have given their all to this MRA movement, working without pay and for long, arduous hours to save the American way of life and to save liberty the world over, I stand in reverent admiration. I am glad that Dr. Buchman is here and that he came over at this time. He has brought with him a task force of three hundred, including sixty-eight representatives from ten European countries who have come with first-hand evidence of the results of this program in increasing production, uniting democratic leadership, and supplying the answering ideology to Communism.

There can be no question as to the very sinister nature of the danger to freedom the world over.

Our worldly materialistic sciences are thousands of centuries ahead of the science of human relations and our spiritual progress. Thus the world is in a most terrible predicament. The people of this nation have not been adequately awakened. The people are entitled to the truth.

Within five years other nations will have the atomic bomb, and when that happens, free nations will be at a very great handicap.

The atomic bomb, due to man's materialism, is here to stay. The problem, therefore, is not the atomic bomb, but human nature itself. It is the evil that lies in human nature that must be conquered. Human nature must be changed. Warlike leaders of nations must be changed.

But time is running out. The clocks are ticking away the hours that bring us near the last fatal hour for civilization. It is later perhaps than we think.

It takes time to change human nature and to rid the world of warlike tyrannical leaders, so those leaders must be held in leash and in check until man can learn to fit himself into this atomic bomb environment that he has created.

The whole human race must be united by integrating it behind a common global purpose by means of a workable method. That is what the atomic era calls for and this program gives you the chance you have been looking for to go into action to help save civilization. This movement strengthens the moral arm of the peace-loving and freedom-loving leaders of the world.

I bespeak your active help with this world force of Moral Re-Armament. America is the last great citadel of liberty. I pray for an upsurge of the human spirit behind this movement to unite the human race by integrating it behind a common, global purpose by means of this workable method.

29. LABOR'S DESTINY

•

The 1947 Assembly for Moral Re-Armament at Mackinac Island, Michigan, was attended by seven hundred delegates from every part of the United States and Canada. Among them were a number of national leaders of labor who issued, on August 31, 1947, a manifesto on the future of industry and of democracy. *The New York Times* described this manifesto in an article (September 1, 1947):

Bearing the signatures of a number of national labor leaders of the United States and Canada, a manifesto calling for industry to join its working forces in a pattern of teamwork that would "sell" democracy to the world was presented today to the seven hundred delegates attending the North American Assembly for Moral Re-Armament.

Labor's destiny, the manifesto maintained, could be:

"To make the wealth and work of the world available to all and for the exploitation of none.

"To find abundance in the economics of unselfishness.

"To turn out work of whose quality and quantity we can be proud.

"To find again the fire and conviction of labor's pioneers, that labor led by God can remake the world."

Continuing, the union leaders called on all elements of industry to join with us in the following program:

"To admit our own faults and release the force for teamwork that comes from a change of heart.

"To make the motive of industry the passion to build a new world.

"To make all decisions on the basis of what's right, rather than who's right.

"To set a pattern of teamwork that will 'sell' democracy to the world."

Among those whose names appeared on the document, released to the public on the eve of Labor Day, were:

L. S. Buckmaster, international president of the United Rubber Workers, and a vice-president of the CIO; William C. Doherty, president of the National Association of Letter Carriers, and a vice-president of the AFL; H. W. Fraser, president of the Order of Railway Conductors; Eric Peterson, secretary-treasurer of the International Association of Machinists; Ernest B. Pugh, CIO regional director for Virginia; Archie Virtue, president of the Michigan State Association of Plumbers, AFL; Russell White, president of Oldsmobile Local

652 of the United Automobile Workers, CIO of Lansing;
Charles H. Millard, Canadian director of the United Steelworkers of America; John V. Riffe, international representative of the United Steelworkers of America; and Elroy Rob-
son, vice-president of the Canadian Brotherhood of Railway
Employees and assistant to the president of the Canadian Congress of Labor.

30. AT WORK IN SAN FRANCISCO

•

Gould Lincoln, veteran Washington columnist and
former President of the Gridiron Club, wrote as follows in his "Political Mill," *Washington Evening
Star*, June 30, 1945:

San Francisco: The United Na-
tions Conference closed here on a note of friendly feeling. If
this same feeling can be maintained by the representatives of
the fifty nations which assembled here—and by their peoples
—the success of this great undertaking is assured. . . .

G. Myrrdin Evans of the British delegation, at one of the
final commission sessions, spoke what many of the delegates
have felt. "No machinery, however perfect, will work if it
has no motive power. The only thing that will finally prevent
war is a change in the minds and hearts of men." In the same
vein Dr. Carl J. Hambro, president of the Norwegian Parliament and last president of the League of Nations Assembly,
said, "What is needed most is not new machinery, but a
change of heart. Even the most perfect international constitution can no more give mankind security than the very best
plough in itself can make farming a success."

During the weeks of the conference a group—not in any
way officially connected with the international gathering—

was at work in San Francisco. This was the moral re-armament group headed by Dr. Frank Buchman. The work of the group in past years was familiar to many of the delegates, although to the great majority it was something new. That it had its measure of effect on the conference itself is the testimony given by several of the leaders of conference delegations. It made its influence felt through the presentation of a play, *The Forgotten Factor*, given several times, to which members of thirty or more of the fifty delegations came . . .

One of the performances of the play took place in the theater of the Bohemian Club. In a brief speech of welcome to those delegates who attended, Brigadier General Carlos P. Romulo, head of the Philippine delegation, said: "What you will see on the stage tonight is something that can be transferred to our conference room, and if the same spirit is reflected in the conference room, I know we will present the world with a Charter that will usher in a new world." He added that he had first seen the play himself "against my conscious will" and that he had later remarked: "Every delegate should see this play, by compulsion if necessary."

31. CHALLENGE TO THE CONTEMPORARY WORLD

•

The booklet by the Rev. J. P. Thornton-Duesbery, Principal of Wycliffe Hall and formerly Master of St. Peter's Hall, Oxford, entitled *The Oxford Group, a Brief Account of its Principles and Growth*, contains a foreword contributed by the following: Lord Ammon; Dr. M. E. Aubrey, then General Secretary of the Baptist Union of Great Britain and Ireland; the late Viscount Bennett, former Prime Minister of Canada; Dr. Sidney M. Berry, then Secretary of the Congregational Union of England and Wales; the

Rt. Rev. W. Purves Boyes, then Moderator of the Presbyterian Church of England and Wales; Lord Courthope; Sir John Craig; the late Brigadier-General Sir Richard Fitzpatrick, former Chairman of the British Legion; the Bishop of Lichfield; Dr. J. Scott Lidgett, former President of the Uniting Conference of the Methodist Churches; Sir Lynden Macassey; Dr. John McKenzie, then Moderator of the General Assembly of the Church of Scotland; Sir David Ross; Dr. John White, former Moderator of the Church of Scotland. In their foreword they say:

It has always been true of growing Christian movements that the greater the success they achieve in presenting the old truths of Christianity in a form that challenges the conditions of the contemporary world, the more is criticism, both ill-informed and ill-disposed, directed against them. Often indeed, such criticism is its own tribute to the power of the movement. . . .

Each one of us from our personal knowledge can affirm the Christian purposes of the Oxford Group. Some of us perhaps would be disposed to emphasize even more strongly than Mr. Thornton-Duesbery has done, the value in particular directions of the work which the Group is doing among all sections of the community in bringing Christianity into common life. But on one thing we are agreed, and that is the impressive contribution which the Group is making to the acceptance of the regenerating truths of Christ's religion by persons to whom before they were merely lifeless phrases.

Mr. Thornton-Duesbery also quotes from an address the late Archbishop of Canterbury, Lord Lang of Lambeth, gave to his clergy in July 1934. The Archbishop said:

The Movement is most certainly doing what the Church of Christ exists everywhere to do. It is changing human lives, giving them a new joy and freedom, liberating them from the faults of temper, of domestic relationships, and the like, which have beset them, and giving them a real ardour to communicate to their fellow creatures what God has given them.

In 1938, the Archbishop sent the following message
to Dr. Buchman on his sixtieth birthday:

I would like to send a message of congratulation to Dr. Buchman on the great work which he has been able to achieve in bringing multitudes of human lives in all parts of the world under the transforming power of Christ.

32. AN ALTERNATIVE

•

On October 2, 1950, at the conclusion of the 1950
World Assembly, *The Times*, London, published the
following summary by their Geneva Correspondent:

The General Assembly on Moral Re-Armament, which has been in conference at Caux since June, will end its session to-morrow.

Its purpose has been to outline and develop an alternative ideology to Marxist materialism sufficiently strong to unite the democratic world in answer to the Communist challenge. Some 8,000 delegates representing seventy nations visited the headquarters at Caux during the summer to take part in the discussions. The British delegation included many trade union officials, dock workers from London, Merseyside, and the Clyde, and factory managers.

Two conferences were held within the General Assembly, the one on industrial peace, the other on security and defence. The purpose of the industrial conference was to discuss the infusion of a new dynamic and spiritual force into industrial and political relations. It was remarked that the Communists were adept at influencing trade unions and parliamentary institutions by infiltration and propaganda. While it was not suggested that the same methods should be employed, many suggestions were put forward for new ideas on labour and industrial leadership to provide the workers with a sound alternative to Marxism. The class struggle, it was generally agreed, was out of date, and many delegates derided the notion that trade unions and management were of necessity hostile to one another.

Military Aspect

The military conference had under consideration the ideological aspects of national and international defence. It started from the principle that Powers at war to-day do not fight merely on the military front but on the ideological front as well. It was pointed out by one French general that apart from events in Korea and Indo-China nine nations in Eastern Europe and almost the whole of China had been absorbed without the armies of Russia being militarily involved. Nations called upon to fight must have a cause to fight for and must know what it was—for this the moral re-armament of each country was as necessary as military re-armament.

The problem facing the Moral Re-Armament movement seemed to emerge as the evolution of an ideology with an expansive power greater than that with which the democratic countries are confronted and forceful enough to cross the iron curtain, to be propagated by a world organisation of convinced and trained people.

33. LAUNCHING OF MORAL RE-ARMAMENT

•

On the occasion of his sixtieth birthday in June 1938, at a reception given in his honor in East Ham Town Hall, cradle of the British Labour Movement, Dr. Frank Buchman launched Moral Re-Armament in the following speech:

The world's condition cannot but cause disquiet and anxiety. Hostility piles up between nation and nation, labor and capital, class and class. The cost of bitterness and fear mounts daily. Friction and frustration are undermining our homes.

Is there a remedy that will cure the individual and the nation and give the hope of a speedy and satisfactory recovery?

The remedy may lie in a return to those simple home truths that some of us learned at our mother's knee, and which many of us have forgotten and neglected—honesty, purity, unselfishness, and love.

The crisis is fundamentally a moral one. The nations must re-arm morally. Moral recovery is essentially the forerunner of economic recovery. Imagine a rising tide of absolute honesty and absolute unselfishness sweeping across every country! What would be the effect? What about taxes? Debts? Savings? A wave of absolute unselfishness throughout the nations would be the end of war.

Moral recovery creates not crisis but confidence and unity in every phase of life. How can we precipitate this moral recovery throughout the nations? We need a power strong enough to change human nature and build bridges between man and man, faction and faction. This starts when everyone admits his own faults instead of spotlighting the other fellow's.

God alone can change human nature.

The secret lies in that great forgotten truth that when man listens, God speaks; when man obeys, God acts; when men change, nations change. That power active in a minority can be the solvent of a whole country's problems. Leaders changed, a nation's thinking changed, a world at peace with itself.

"We, the Remakers of the World"—is that not the thinking and willing of the ordinary man? The average man wants to see the other fellow honest, the other nation at peace with his own. We all want to get, but with such changed leaders we might all want to give. We might find in this new spirit an answer to the problems which are paralyzing economic recovery.

Suppose everybody cared enough, everybody shared enough, wouldn't everybody have enough? There is enough in the world for everyone's need, but not enough for everyone's greed.

Think of the unemployed thus released for a program of Moral Re-Armament; everyone in the nation magnetized and mobilized to restore the nations to security, safety, and sanity.

Every man, woman, and child must be enlisted; every home become a fort. Our aim should be that everyone has not only enough of the necessities of life, but that he has a legitimate part in bringing about this Moral Re-Armament, and so safeguards the peace of his nation and the peace of the world.

God has a nation-wide program that provides inspiration and liberty for all and anticipates all political programs.

Every employed and unemployed man employed in Moral Re-Armament; this is the greatest program of national service —putting everybody to work remaking people, homes, and businesses. A Swedish steelworker told me: "Only a spiritual revolution goes far enough to meet the needs of men and industry."

A Labour leader said: "I have seen the Labour Movement triumph and felt in the midst of triumph an emptiness. The Oxford Group gave my life new content. I see in its message the only key to the future of the Labour Movement and of industry the world over."

Only a new spirit in men can bring a new spirit in industry. Industry can be the pioneer of a new order, where national service replaces selfishness, and where industrial planning is based upon the guidance of God. When Labor, Management, and Capital become partners under God's guidance, then industry takes its true place in national life.

New men, new homes, new industry, new nations, a new world.

⌈We have not yet tapped the great creative sources in the Mind of God. God has a plan, and the combined moral and spiritual forces of the nation can find that plan.⌉

We can, we must, and we will generate a moral and spiritual force that is powerful enough to remake the world.

34. WHAT ARE YOU LIVING FOR?

•

This address by Dr. Buchman was given on his birthday, June 4, 1950, at a reception in his honor at the Hans Sachs Haus, Gelsenkirchen, Germany.

The gathering marked the climax of the twelfth-anniversary celebrations of Moral Re-Armament held in the Ruhr at the invitation of five Minister-Presidents, including Herr Karl Arnold of North Rhine-Westphalia, then President of the Upper House of the Federal Parliament, and with the warm support of Dr. Adenauer, the Chancellor.

Twelve years ago I walked in the woods of the Black Forest near Freudenstadt. The world was on the edge of chaos. Just as today, everyone longed for peace and prepared for war.

As I walked in those quiet woods one thought kept coming

to me—"moral and spiritual re-armament, moral and spiritual re-armament. The next great movement in the world will be a movement of moral re-armament for all nations."

A few days later I was in London in the East End where the British Labour Movement began. The workers responded. Moral Re-Armament went to the world. The newspapers carried it, the radio. Today, twelve years later, in many parts of the world people are gathering to plan for the Moral Re-Armament of their nations. The London workers are meeting in Poplar Town Hall with the dockers. In Birmingham Town Hall labor and management from the British heavy industries and the coal mines are celebrating the day, and in Glasgow the Clydeside shipworkers.

In America my friends will be speaking on a two-way telephone conversation, giving us news of the advance in America and hearing the news of what you have been doing here in Germany.

Messages have been coming in the last few days from Australia and New Zealand, from India, South Africa, America, from all parts of Europe, from Japan and the Far East. Typical of many is the following from the executive head of the Government Planning Commission of India, Gulzarilal Nanda: "Greetings from those of us who have pinned our faith on MRA to cure the ills of the world. Each year MRA is growing in world significance and in power. MRA will not have done its job till the ideology it represents becomes the most significant and the most powerful factor in political, economic, and social thought and action in every part of the world."

What is the secret behind the triumph of a God-given thought? What is it that has enabled an ordinary man like myself and hundreds of thousands of men and women across the world to do the extraordinary thing? Only the very selfish or the very blind person is content to leave the world as it is today. Most of us would like to change the world. The trouble is, too many of us want to do it our own way. Some people have the right diagnosis but they bring the wrong cure. They reckon without God and without a change in human nature, and the result is confusion, bitterness, and war. Other people are quite sure they have the answer in theory, but they always want somebody else or some other nation to begin. The result is frustration and despair.

(When the right diagnosis and the right cure come together, the result is a miracle. Human nature changes and human society changes.)

Let me illustrate this with a personal word because it happened to me one day forty-two years ago. For the first time I saw myself with all my pride, my selfishness, my failure, and my sin. "I" was the center of my own life. If I was to be different, then that big "I" had to be crossed out.

I saw the resentments I had against six men standing out like tombstones in my heart.

I asked God to change me and He told me to put things right with those six men. I obeyed God and wrote six letters of apology.

The same day God used me to change another man's life. I saw that when I obeyed God, miracles happened. I learnt the truth that when man listens, God speaks; when man obeys, God acts; when men change, nations change.

That was the revolutionary path I set my feet on forty-two years ago, which millions are treading now, and on which I challenge you to join me today.

What are you living for? What is your nation living for? Selfish men and selfish nations can drag the world to total disaster. A new type of man, a new type of statesmanship, a new type of national policy—that is our instant need, and this is the purpose for which Moral Re-Armament has come to birth.

A young Swiss engineer, successful in his profession, with family, friends, position, and wealth, died this spring. He had discovered this same secret of investing his life and his possessions to create a new world based on change. He gave himself with his wife, who is with us today, and with his children, to make Caux the world center it has become for all nations. Suddenly people have realized that in five short years he accomplished more for the world than many men in their whole lives.

This young Swiss followed in the steps of another young man who, seven hundred years ago, put aside fame and career and gave everything he had to change the world. He brought a new life to Europe and his life has inspired countless millions since then. He was St. Francis of Assisi. This young Swiss engineer, so his wife tells me, kept constantly by him these words of St. Francis; and they are the secret of how to change the world.

Lord, make me the instrument of Your peace.
Where there is hatred may I bring love;
Where there is malice may I bring pardon;
Where there is discord may I bring harmony;
Where there is error may I bring truth;
Where there is doubt may I bring faith;
Where there is despair may I bring hope;
Where there is darkness may I bring Your light;
Where there is sadness may I bring joy.

O, Master, may I seek not so much to be comforted as to comfort,
To be understood as to understand,
To be loved as to love,
For it is in giving that we receive,
It is in losing our lives that we shall find them,
It is in forgiving that we shall be forgiven,
It is in dying that we shall rise up to eternal life.

The collected speeches of Dr. Frank N. D. Buchman are available under the title of Remaking the World, *which is now published in Chinese, Danish, Dutch, English, French, German, Italian, Japanese, Norwegian, and Swedish.*

INDEX

Further information about Moral Re-Armament can be obtained from:

MORAL RE-ARMAMENT

833 South Flower Street　　640 Fifth Avenue
Los Angeles 17, California　　New York 19, New York

Box 38, Station F
PB 4655 Toronto, Ontario, Canada